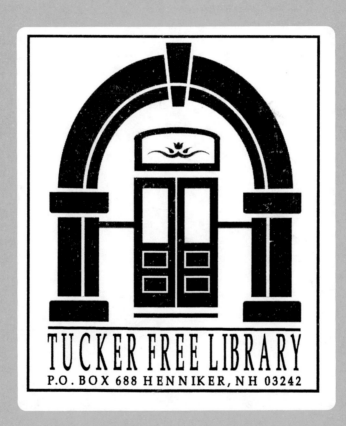

STEP-BY-STEP
Cake
Decorating

STEP-BY-STEP
Cake Decorating

Karen Sullivan

LONDON, NEW YORK, MELBOURNE,
MUNICH, AND DELHI

DK UK
Project Editor Martha Burley
Project Art Editor Kathryn Wilding
Managing Editor Dawn Henderson
Managing Art Editor Christine Keilty
Senior Jacket Creative Nicola Powling
Jacket Design Assistant Rosie Levine
Producer, Pre-Production Sarah Isle
Producers David Appleyard, Jen Scothern
Art Director Peter Luff
Publisher Peggy Vance

Cake Decorators Asma Hassan,
Sandra Monger, Amelia Nutting

DK US
US Senior Editor Rebecca Warren
US Editor Margaret Parrish
North American Consultant Kate Ramos

DK INDIA
Senior Editor Charis Bhagianathan
Senior Art Editors Ira Sharma, Balwant Singh
Editor Janashree Singha
Assistant Art Editors Tanya Mehrotra, Aastha Tiwari
Managing Editor Alicia Ingty
Managing Art Editor Navidita Thapa
Production Manager Pankaj Sharma
Pre-Production Manager Sunil Sharma
Senior DTP Designer Jagtar Singh
DTP Designers Satish Chandra Gaur,
Rajdeep Singh, Rajesh Singh, Sachin Singh,
Anurag Trivedi, Manish Upreti

13 14 15 16 17   10 9 8 7 6 5 4 3 2 1
001—193751—Oct/2013

First American Edition, 2013
Published in the United States by DK Publishing,
4th Floor, 345 Hudson Street, New York, New York 10014

A catalog record for this book is available from the Library of Congress.
ISBN: 978-1-4654-1441-0

DK books are available for special discounts when purchased in bulk
for sales promotions, premiums, fund-raising, or educational use.
For details, contact: DK Publishing Special Markets; 4th Floor, 345
Hudson Street, New York, New York 10014 or SpecialSales@DK.com

Color reproduction by Altaimage LTD
Printed and bound in South China

Discover more at **www.dk.com**

Contents

Introduction

CAKE DECORATING has enjoyed a huge surge in interest over the last few years, with enthusiastic beginners creating celebration cakes, exquisite cupcakes, and perfect cake pops in their own homes. This trend is possible thanks to the multitude of tools and specialty ingredients that are now available, and the help of decorating classes, blogs, websites, online videos, books, and programs that are devoted to the subject. We are no longer afraid to bake, and our creations are becoming more sophisticated and adventurous as time goes on. But how do we get started? What do we need to know to create beautifully decorated cakes with that perfect finish?

This is the ideal book for anyone who wants to learn how to make spectacular cakes of their own. With its unique user-friendly structure, detailed step-by-step instructions, and exciting projects, it guides and inspires as you master the basics.

An introductory illustrated **Tools and equipment** section shows you what you need to know to streamline and enhance the process of decorating cakes. Get started with a chapter devoted to techniques for preparing and using your **Key ingredients**, such as gum paste, marzipan,

fondant, buttercream frosting, tempered chocolate, and royal icing to pipe or frost. Continue with over 100 clear step-by-step **Decorating techniques**— all of which include tips from the experts to make the techniques failsafe and achievable. With over 20 simply glorious **Projects** from three award-winning cake designers, you'll find everything you need to make special celebration cakes with great success. Finally, in an expansive **Cake basics** chapter, there are delicious recipes for cakes in a wide variety of flavors, textures, shapes, and sizes, and instructions for making them work—every time.

Like all skills, cake decorating can take some time to learn and a little patience to master. Some techniques are simple, others require practice. All, however, will help you to create original cakes, cupcakes, 3-D creations, and cake pops that are sure to thrill your family and friends.

Happy decorating!

Decoration planners
Floral

Ruffled cake
pp.224–25

Filigree wedding cake
pp.214–16

Blossom stencil cake
pp.205–07

Cupcake bouquet
pp.198–99

Cigarillo wedding cake
pp.210–12

Wedding mini cakes
p.213

Heart-shaped posy cake
pp.200–01

Gerbera

Cymbidium orchid

Orchids, cornflowers,
and baby's breath

Purple roses

Creating flowers and sprays
pp.90–91

Butterflies and blossoms
pp.184–85

Children's

Princess cake pops
p.175

Teddy bear mini cakes
pp.190–91

Princess castle
pp.170–75

Dinosaur cake
pp.167–69

Train cake
pp.164–66

Pirate cake pops
p.179

Scary cake pops
p.189

Halloween pumpkin cake
pp.186–88

Rabbit

Cow

Baby ladybug

Teddy bear

Pirate ship cake
pp.176–79

Modeling characters
pp.94–95

Novelty

Handbag cake
pp.202–04

Sports' ball cakes
pp.180–82

Suitcase cake
pp.208–09

Gingerbread house
pp.194–95

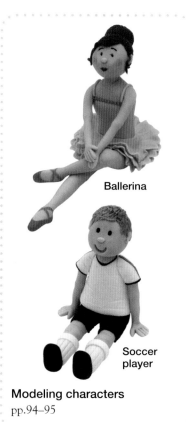

Ballerina

Soccer player

Modeling characters
pp.94–95

Elegant

Shades of pink
pp.196–97

Blossom stencil cake
pp.205–07

Cigarillo wedding cake
pp.210–12

Ruffled cake
pp.224–25

Calla spray

Creating flowers and sprays
pp.90–91

Damask

Stencil designs
pp.132–33

Occasions

Christmas cake pops
p.223

Newborn celebration cake
pp.192–93

Filigree wedding cake
pp.214–16

Halloween pumpkin cake
pp.186–88

Festive yule log
pp.218–19

Cigarillo wedding cake
pp.210–12

Festive fruitcake
pp.220–22

Poinsettia

Creating flowers and sprays
pp.90–91

Tumbling teddy bears

Stencil designs
pp.132–33

Valentine's hearts

Festive stars

Plunger cutter designs
pp.104–05

Tools and equipment

Almost all of the different effects, textures, decorative touches and, indeed, perfect finishes for professional cakes rely on the use of specialty, widely available tools and equipment. Assembling a toolkit of these essentials can make cake decorating so much easier.

Baking and assembling

Prepare a flawless cake with the help of specialty tools for baking, frosting, stacking, and presenting.

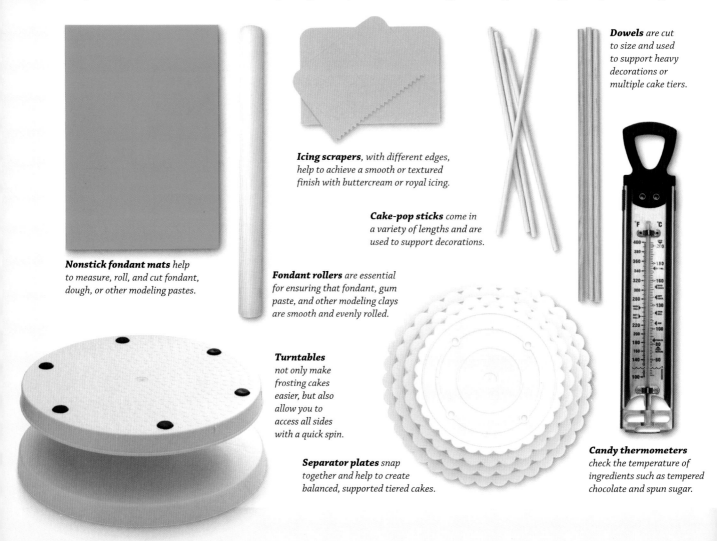

Dowels *are cut to size and used to support heavy decorations or multiple cake tiers.*

Icing scrapers, *with different edges, help to achieve a smooth or textured finish with buttercream or royal icing.*

Cake-pop sticks *come in a variety of lengths and are used to support decorations.*

Nonstick fondant mats *help to measure, roll, and cut fondant, dough, or other modeling pastes.*

Fondant rollers *are essential for ensuring that fondant, gum paste, and other modeling clays are smooth and evenly rolled.*

Turntables *not only make frosting cakes easier, but also allow you to access all sides with a quick spin.*

Separator plates *snap together and help to create balanced, supported tiered cakes.*

Candy thermometers *check the temperature of ingredients such as tempered chocolate and spun sugar.*

Pillars separate and provide support for cake tiers. They come in many different styles.

Fondant smoothers smooth decorations, boards, or cake toppings. Use two to achieve crisp corners and edges.

Cake levelers ensure a perfectly level cake and allow you to even out domes and other mistakes made while baking.

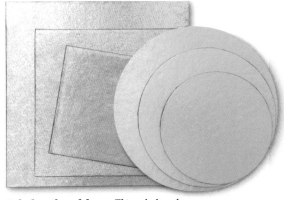

Cake boards and drums Thin cake boards support individual cakes for multiple tiers. Thicker drums provide a sturdy base.

Molding and embossing

Use one of a number of different molds to produce two- and three-dimensional decorations, and decorate the surface of cakes and decorations with the use of embossers.

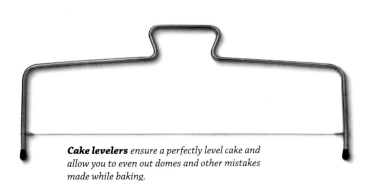

Resin molds ensure that detailed decorations, such as lace or facial features made from fondant or modeling pastes, hold their shape.

Crimpers add design features, decorative shapes, and texture to fondant.

Veiners help emboss veins and provide shape to fondant or gum paste leaves.

Embossing mats are used for rolling fondant. Press the paste into the surface for a variety of textures.

Silicone molds are used for chocolate, gum paste, and fondant.

Plastic molds are ideal for large creations, especially those made from tempered chocolate.

Embossing rollers are used to emboss the surface of decorations or fondant cake coverings.

Cutting

It is easy to cut both detailed and simple shapes accurately with the help of specialty cutters. Many play a dual role by embossing at the same time.

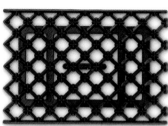

Plunger cutters *create crisp shapes that are released with the touch of a button. Some also emboss the surface.*

Patchwork cutters *help emboss the surface of cakes and decorations, or cut out detailed designs that can be painted, dusted, or layered.*

Multi-ribbon cutters *make cutting accurate lengths and strips of fondant or other pastes easy. Choose the width and attach interchangeable cutters that can emboss and/or cut decorative edges.*

Tappit cutters *are perfect for small, detailed decorations. They can cut out fine shapes like letters and numbers and emboss a design on the surface.*

Cutting wheels *help cut fondant, gum paste, and other pastes quickly, easily, and accurately. Many come with multiple heads for different effects.*

Metal cutters *help cut accurate shapes that can be layered or used as the basis for decorations. Many come in sets of multiple sizes.*

Modeling

Adding detail and modeling decorations is easy with the help of many tools that can create different effects. You can purchase the essential tools (see opposite) in a set.

Flower formers *allow you to dry fondant or gum-paste flowers and other decorations in a concave shape, and support your creations as you apply detail to the surface.*

Flower picks *are hygienic tools to help you insert fresh or wired floral decorations into the surface of a cake.*

Flower nails *provide control while piping. Rotate one between your thumb and forefinger to turn it as you pipe flowers onto the surface.*

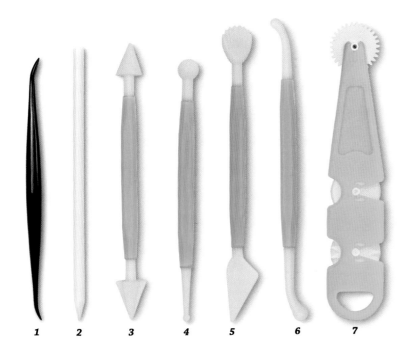

1 Veining tools, also known as Dresden tools, add detail to fondant or paste decorations.

2 Frilling tools can be rolled across thinly rolled fondant to create frills and ruffles.

3 Cone tools create detail and texture. They double as star embossers.

4 Ball tools can thin and soften edges to create natural petal shapes and contours.

5 Scallop tools help to emboss shell patterns and textures and cut shell shapes.

6 Bone tools smooth curves when modeling, and cup and frill flower petals.

7 Stitching (quilting) wheel tools emboss decorations and cakes with stitching effects.

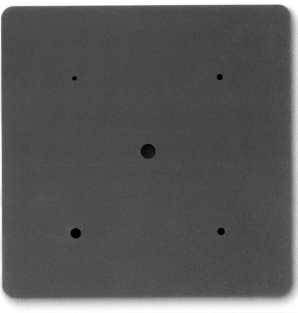

Floral wire comes in a variety of different "gauges." Use it to produce sprays of decorations, such as hearts or stars, and to wire flowers and foliage.

Floral tape is used to cover the surface of floral wire. Tape together wires to create stunning displays of flowers and leaves.

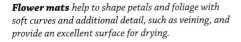

Flower mats help to shape petals and foliage with soft curves and additional detail, such as veining, and provide an excellent surface for drying.

Piping

Piping can be used for a wide range of decorative work, including frosting cupcakes, lettering, trimming, and embroidering. Build up a collection of tips (also known as nozzles) to make decorating easier.

Round tips *are versatile and widely used. They come in many sizes, from tiny tips for piping dots, embroidery, and lettering, to wider tips for prominent effects.*

Petal tips *are available in many sizes and help to create realistic flower petals, as well as ruffles, drapes, swags, and bows with royal icing or buttercream frosting.*

Couplers *allow you to change tips without emptying the piping bag.*

Closed star tips *help to pipe ruffles on cupcakes or mini cakes, as well as buttercream swirls and shells.*

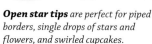

Open star tips *are perfect for piped borders, single drops of stars and flowers, and swirled cupcakes.*

Piping bags *come in a variety of sizes. Choose larger ones to pipe buttercream frosting on cakes or cupcakes, and smaller ones for more detailed work with royal icing.*

Leaf tips *have V-shaped openings, perfect for pointed ends on leaves. Pipe them flat, ruffled, or as 3-D creations.*

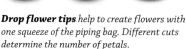

Drop flower tips *help to create flowers with one squeeze of the piping bag. Different cuts determine the number of petals.*

Shell and rope tips *are used to create ropes and shell borders in varying sizes, scrolls, and other borders.*

Multi-opening tips *are ideal for stranded details or beads, as well as scallops.*

Basketweave tips *are serrated on one side to make ribbed, wide stripes of frosting.*

Ruffle tips *have a teardrop-like opening that produces a range of ribbons, swags, and ruffles.*

Piping bottles *with small tips help to pipe chocolate and thinner royal icing, or to drizzle designs on the surface of cakes, cookies, and cake pops.*

Painting

Use pens, edible dusts, inks, and even glitter to add color, create detail, and add an exquisite finish to your cakes and decorations. Paint freehand or with the help of stencils or an airbrushing machine.

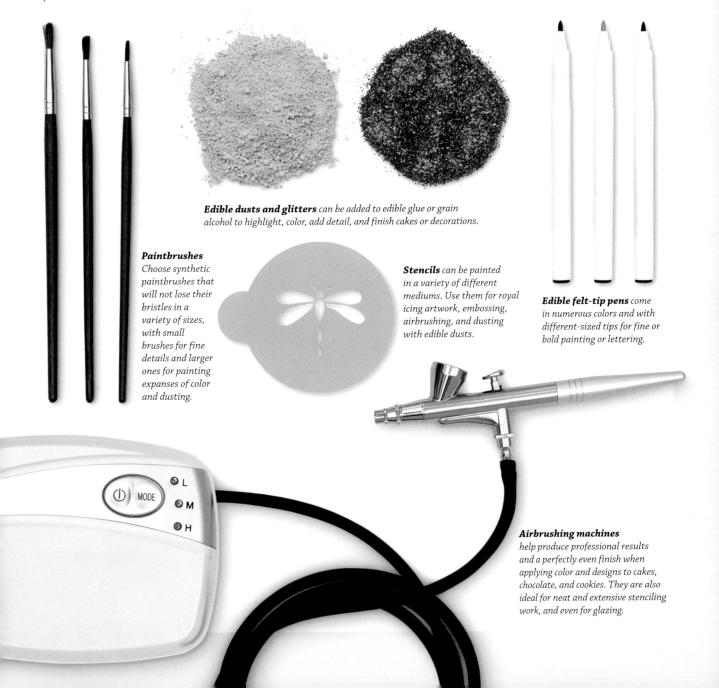

Edible dusts and glitters *can be added to edible glue or grain alcohol to highlight, color, add detail, and finish cakes or decorations.*

Paintbrushes
Choose synthetic paintbrushes that will not lose their bristles in a variety of sizes, with small brushes for fine details and larger ones for painting expanses of color and dusting.

Stencils *can be painted in a variety of different mediums. Use them for royal icing artwork, embossing, airbrushing, and dusting with edible dusts.*

Edible felt-tip pens *come in numerous colors and with different-sized tips for fine or bold painting or lettering.*

Airbrushing machines
help produce professional results and a perfectly even finish when applying color and designs to cakes, chocolate, and cookies. They are also ideal for neat and extensive stenciling work, and even for glazing.

KEY INGREDIENTS

A few basic ingredients form the building blocks of cake decorating.
Find out how to prepare these ingredients, flavor or color them
to your preference, and use them to frost, cover, and texture a cake.

Buttercream frosting

This type of frosting is made with butter, confectioner's sugar, and cream or milk, and is lightly flavored with vanilla or another flavoring. Use it to frost and fill sponge cakes and cupcakes. Some buttercreams require cooking, but most can be whipped up quickly with an electric mixer.

Basic vanilla buttercream frosting

You can make this with or without cream or milk. It is ideal for crumb-coating, frosting sponge cakes, and for piping onto cupcakes. You can also use it for brushwork embroidery (see p.139).

 PREP 15–20 mins

 MAKES 3 cups

Ingredients

* just over 1 cup unsalted butter, softened
* 2 tsp vanilla extract
* 3 cups confectioner's sugar
* 2 tbsp heavy cream or milk, plus extra for thinning
* coloring paste, optional

1 Cream the butter and vanilla together with an electric mixer. Beat in the confectioner's sugar.

2 Beat in the cream and continue mixing until the frosting is light and fluffy.

3 Transfer to a bowl and add coloring paste, a little at a time, until you get the right color.

4 The frosting should be firm enough to hold a knife upright, but soft enough to be piped.

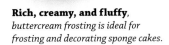

Rich, creamy, and fluffy, *buttercream frosting is ideal for frosting and decorating sponge cakes.*

Variations

For flavored buttercreams, replace the vanilla with another natural extract, such as a nut or fruit extract. Try flavor pairings such as mint and chocolate. You can even use pure oils, such as lemon, orange, or lavender. Start with 1 drop and taste before adding more.

Ingredients

For chocolate buttercream

* basic ingredients (see opposite) plus:
* ½ cup cocoa powder

For lemon or orange buttercream

* basic ingredients (see opposite) plus:
* finely grated zest and juice of 1 lemon or 1 orange

For coffee buttercream

* basic ingredients (see opposite) plus:
* 2 tbsp strong coffee, such as espresso, cooled

For cream cheese buttercream

* basic ingredients (see opposite) plus:
* 7oz (200g) full-fat cream cheese, softened

Chocolate buttercream

This frosting works well with dark chocolate cakes. Follow steps 1–2 of the basic vanilla buttercream recipe. Add the cocoa powder and beat until fluffy. Use milk instead of cream in step 2, and beat until smooth. If you prefer a lighter flavor, halve the amount of cocoa powder. Add it in at step 1, before you start beating.

Lemon or orange buttercream

This zesty buttercream is perfect on a vanilla sponge cake. Follow step 1 of the basic vanilla buttercream recipe, omitting the vanilla. Instead of adding cream, use lemon or orange juice in step 2, beating until smooth. Add the lemon or orange zest, mixing continuously.

Coffee buttercream

This frosting has a light coffee flavor that can be deepened by using stronger coffee. Follow step 1 of the basic vanilla buttercream recipe. Use only 1 tablespoon of cream and add the coffee, beating until evenly distributed, light, and fluffy. For a slightly marbled appearence, beat in 2 tbsp coffee powder instead.

Cream cheese buttercream

This frosting is looser and creamier than a basic buttercream, but sets nicely. Follow step 1 of the basic vanilla buttercream recipe. Omit the cream and add the cream cheese, a little at a time, beating vigorously until fluffy. Keep 2 cups of extra confectioner's sugar on hand and add more to achieve the desired consistency.

Italian meringue buttercream

Rich, smooth, soft, and creamy, meringue buttercreams can be flavored with extracts or a dash of citrus oil. Egg-based buttercreams like this are tricky to make and are too soft for detailed piping. The end result is well worth the effort, however, since they are great for piping cupcakes.

 PREP 25 mins

 COOK 15 mins

 MAKES 2 cups

Equipment

* candy thermometer

Ingredients

* 5 large free-range pasteurized egg whites
* 1¼ cups granulated sugar
* 2¼ cups unsalted butter, softened
* flavoring, optional

1 Place the egg whites in the bowl of an electric mixer and beat with a mixer until foamy with soft peaks. Beat in ¼ cup of the sugar, a little at a time, and mix until firm peaks appear.

2 In a medium pan, add the remaining granulated sugar and ⅓ cup water and heat over low heat. Swirl the pan gently to help the sugar melt and then turn up the heat to medium. Bring to a boil and cook until the candy thermometer reaches 250°F (121°C). Remove from the heat.

3 Continue to beat the egg mixture, using the lowest setting, and pour in the sugar syrup, running it down the side of the bowl. When the bowl is cool to the touch, add the butter, 1 teaspoon at a time. Keep beating. If the mix is runny, keep adding butter until smooth and stiff. Stir in flavoring, if using.

Variations

Try other buttercream frostings: German buttercream involves making a pastry cream by heating eggs, milk, sugar, and cornstarch, straining, and then beating in butter. French buttercream is richer, using egg yolks rather than whites.

Italian meringue buttercream *should be smooth and stiff. Add flavors when the texture is right.*

Rolled buttercream

Rolled buttercream is a softer, shinier type of malleable frosting. It has similarities in texture to traditional fondant, but it is so much tastier. It can be flavored with cocoa powder, if desired, used to cover cakes and cookies, and strengthened for decorations (see p.87).

 PREP 20 mins

 MAKES 4½ cups

Equipment

* dough hook, optional

Ingredients

* just over 1 cup unsalted butter, softened
* 1 cup corn syrup
* ½ tsp salt
* 1 tsp pure vanilla extract
* 5 cups confectioner's sugar, plus extra for dusting

1 In a large bowl, beat together the butter and corn syrup until smooth and well-blended. Mix in the salt and vanilla extract. Gradually mix in the confectioner's sugar, a little at a time, until the frosting becomes stiff.

2 If you have a dough hook, attach it now and use it to knead the frosting until pliable and smooth. If the frosting is sticky, add a little more confectioner's sugar.

3 If you do not have a dough hook, turn the frosting onto a board dusted with confectioner's sugar and knead by hand.

4 To use, roll the frosting out to the required thickness on a clean surface dusted with confectioner's sugar. Apply to cakes or use to decorate in the same ways as fondant (see pp.46–51).

Tip
Rolled buttercream does not keep as long as traditional fondant. It needs to be stored in the refrigerator in an airtight container. Before rolling, warm it gently with your hands and knead on a surface dusted with confectioner's sugar.

A dough hook *can help with the effort of kneading rolled buttercream.*

Filling a layer cake

Cake layers always need to be leveled before they are filled (see p.239). Sandwiching thin layers makes a sponge cake sturdier and eaiser to carve. Ganache (see p.38) can also be used to fill cakes, as can whipped cream, jam, and fruit curds. Avoid overfilling, and allow the filling to set before frosting.

Equipment
* cake board
* turntable or lazy Susan
* piping bag with large, round tip

Ingredients
* cooled cake layers, leveled
* buttercream frosting (see pp.24–25)

1 Place the base layer and board on a turntable, leveled-side up. Fill the piping bag with frosting and pipe around the inside edge.

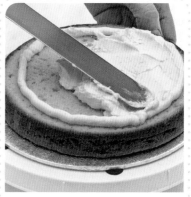

2 Using a spoon, place a large dollop of frosting in the center and spread to the edges with a palette knife, until smooth.

Cake layers always need to be leveled before filling

3 Place the next layer on top, leveled-side down. For 2-layered cakes, you are now ready to crumb-coat and frost. To build the cake higher, repeat, with the next layer leveled-side up and then the leveled-side down. You could finish with a leveled-side down layer, for a level surface.

LAYERING CAKES
Carving and covering cakes **p.65**
Building tiered cakes **p.68**
Building with pillars **p.69**

Crumb-coating a cake

Crumb-coating is like adding primer to a wall before painting it. It helps to ensure a perfect finish for frosted or fondant-covered cakes. It smoothes over any cracks or holes in the surface and helps the cake stay sealed and moist. You can crumb-coat with buttercream or, if desired, ganache (see p.38).

Equipment
* cake board
* turntable or lazy Susan

Ingredients
* cakes, leveled, and layers filled with buttercream frosting
* buttercream frosting (see pp.24–25), thinned with some milk

...ensure a perfect finish for frosted cakes

CRUMB-COATING CAKES

Carving and covering cakes **p.65**
Building tiered cakes **p.68**
Building with pillars **p.69**
Building asymmetrical cakes **pp.70–71**

1 Place the cake on a board, on a turntable. Using a palette knife, carefully apply a thin layer of buttercream to the cake.

2 Start at the top of the cake and swirl the buttercream over the surface as you turn it around on the turntable.

3 Spread the frosting around the sides until evenly covered. A few crumbs may be embedded in the frosting; this is normal.

4 Refrigerate or allow to dry for up to 2 hours. Apply the final layer of frosting (see pp.30–31) or fondant (see p.50).

Frosting a cake

This method works best of all with buttercream frosting, although you could use ganache (see p.38) or whipped cream. Use tools, such as serrated scrapers, to create a variety of textures as you frost. A textured look can be achieved by spreading the frosting in swirls, rather than smoothing with a hot knife.

Equipment

* cake board
* turntable or lazy Susan
* untextured paper towels
* scraper, flat-edged

Ingredients

* buttercream frosting (see pp.24–25)
* cake, leveled, layered, and crumb-coated (see p.29)

...achieve a textured look by spreading the frosting in swirls

FROSTING CAKES

1 Dot a small amount of buttercream on the cake board and center the cake on top. Place on a turntable and dollop a large amount of buttercream into the center of the cake.

2 With a palette knife, swirl and smooth the frosting, spreading it outward and over the sides as you go.

3 Turn the cake as you spread the frosting down and around the sides of the cake, to cover it as evenly as possible. When it is smooth, allow the cake to set for about 10 minutes, and then repeat.

4 Fill a mug with boiling water and insert a palette knife blade into it. When it is hot, dry it and run it around the sides, turning the cake around with the flat surface of the knife against the frosting. Repeat until smooth.

5 Make the top smooth with a hot knife, turning the cake with the flat surface of the knife against the frosting. Move from one side of the cake to the other. Allow the cake to set for about 15 minutes.

6 Place a sheet of untextured paper towel on the surface and "polish" the cake so that the surface is smooth. Use a scraper to smooth the frosting all the way around the cake, if desired.

Piping cupcakes

You can frost a cupcake with buttercream frosting using a palette knife, rotating it on a flat surface as you spread. For a quick, professional-looking finish, however, pipe the buttercream into a swirl, as shown here. Use different tips for stars, shells, or a variety of effects and textures.

Equipment

* piping bag with large open-star tip

Ingredients

* buttercream frosting (see pp.24–25)
* cooled cupcakes
* sprinkles or edible glitter, optional

...use different tips for a variety of effects and textures

PIPING WITH BUTTERCREAM

Making a piping bag **p.73**
Filling a piping bag **p.74**
Piping buttercream borders **p.78**
Piping a buttercream rose **p.79**
Piping lettering **p.84**

1 Attach the tip to the piping bag and fill it half full with medium-consistency frosting. More makes the bag difficult to handle.

2 Hold the tip ½in (1cm) above the cupcake, at a 90° angle, and pipe from the outside edge inward, in a spiral.

3 Apply pressure so that an even quantity is released. Slowly increase the pressure at the center, so that the frosting forms a peak.

4 Release the pressure to end the spiral at the center of the cupcake. Decorate with sprinkles or edible glitter, if desired.

Filling cupcakes

Cupcakes can be filled with jam, buttercream frosting, ganache, cream, or even loosened peanut butter, fruit mousses, and fruit curds. Add in a marshmallow or another treat before filling, for an extra surprise. There are two successful methods for filling cakes with liquid ingredients.

Cone method

With a sharp paring knife, cut out a cone shape from the center of each cupcake. Slice off the tip of the cone, fill the cone-shaped cavity in the cupcake to just below the top, and then replace the flat end of the cone on top. Proceed to frost as usual (see opposite).

Piping method

If you have thin, smooth frosting or jam, you can use a plain round tip (pictured below) or a specialized injector tip on a piping bag. Attach the tip, load the piping bag with filling, and then insert it into the center of the cupcake, from the top. Gently press on the bag until the filling begins to expand out of the insertion hole. Proceed to frost and decorate as usual (see opposite).

Using a piping bag *will help to control the amount of filling you use.*

> ### Tip
> *Always make sure the cupcakes are completely cool before attempting to fill them or they will fall apart. Cooling will also ensure that the filling will not melt into the cupcake, making it soggy and messy to eat.*

Royal icing

Make this sweet icing with egg whites, confectioner's sugar, and lemon juice. Traditionally, it is used to ice Christmas fruitcakes and to decorate gingerbread houses. With a few changes to the recipe, it can be used for decorative piping (see pp.73–75) and "run-outs" (see pp.140–41).

Traditional royal icing

Royal icing dries hard, so keep it covered with plastic wrap or a damp towel while you are working. The glycerine in this recipe stops the icing from becoming rock hard and provides a little shine.

 PREP 15 mins

 MAKES 3¼ cups

Equipment

✳ scraper or serrated
   scraper, optional

Ingredients

✳ 3 large free-range
   pasteurized egg whites;
   or albumen powder,
   mixed with water
✳ 6 cups confectioner's
   sugar, sifted
✳ 1 tsp lemon juice
✳ 2 tsp glycerine
✳ fruitcake, leveled and
   layered if desired,
   covered with marzipan

1 Beat the egg whites in a bowl until foamy. Add confectioner's sugar, a spoonful at a time.

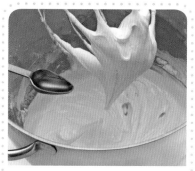

2 Stir in the lemon juice and glycerine, then beat until stiff and peaks begin to form.

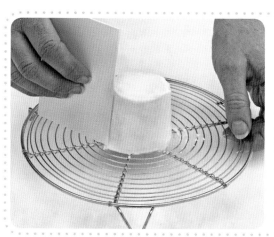

To ice a cake, add more confectioner's sugar to thicken, if necessary. Use a palette knife to spread on the top and sides of your cake, as with buttercream frosting (see pp.30–31). Use a scraper, as shown with a mini cake, for a smooth finish. Try a serrated scraper for a uniform texture.

Whipped into a smooth icing or thickened for piping, royal icing provides an elegant finishing touch to a special cake.

Tip

Fill the piping bag with royal icing (see p.74) and keep the remainder covered. The icing will last up to 2 weeks, so long as it is well covered and refrigerated, but you may need to mix and thicken it with confectioner's sugar before using.

Royal icing for piping

This recipe is very similar to traditional royal icing, but it does not contain glycerine. This makes it more appropriate for detailed piping work and gingerbread houses, when it needs to dry hard.

PREP 20 mins

MAKES 2½ cups

Ingredients

* 3 large free-range pasteurized egg whites
* 1 tsp lemon juice, plus extra if needed
* 6 cups confectioner's sugar, sifted
* coloring paste, optional

PIPING WITH ROYAL ICING

Building with gingerbread **pp.66–67**

Basic royal icing piping **p.75**

Piping dots, beads, and flowers **p.80**

1 Beat the egg whites in a bowl. Stir in the lemon juice. Slowly add the confectioner's sugar.

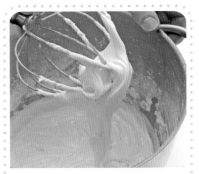

2 Continue to beat until the icing has a smooth consistency like toothpaste.

3 Add more lemon juice if it is too thick. Dip a toothpick into the coloring paste, if using. Add just a dot of coloring paste at a time—a little goes a long way. Mix into the royal icing and stir until you achieve a uniform color.

Marzipan

Marzipan is a thick, sweet almond paste that is traditionally used to cover fruitcakes underneath royal icing or fondant. It is also a great medium for modeling and even molding decorations for cakes. Its high sugar content allows it to last for months without refrigeration.

 PREP 20 mins   **MAKES** 2lb (900g)

Ingredients

* ¾ cup granulated sugar
* 2½ cups confectioner's sugar, sifted, plus extra for rolling and kneading
* 4 cups ground almonds
* 1 tsp pure vanilla extract
* ½ tsp orange juice
* 2 large eggs, beaten

Tips

Marzipan can be colored in the same way as fondant (see p.47). Knead a dab of coloring paste into the marzipan. Marzipan has a soft texture and will dry hard without a strengthener. Keep decorations in an airtight container once dry.

1 Mix both the sugars and ground almonds in a bowl. Make a well in the center and add the vanilla extract, orange juice, and eggs.

2 Use a palette knife to fold the wet ingredients gently into the dry ingredients, until you have a crumbly dough.

3 Dust a flat surface with confectioner's sugar, and knead the marzipan until smooth. Add more confectioner's sugar, if needed, to get the right consistency.

Almond-rich marzipan provides a succulent layer of sweetness on fruitcakes. You can model it into a variety of shapes.

Tip

Apricot glaze seals cakes and provides a sheen. It is made by mixing ¾ cup of apricot jam with 3 tablespoons of water. Gently heat in a small pan until warm and stir in 1 tablespoon of brandy. Strain, and brush onto cakes.

Covering a cake with marzipan

Traditionally, fruitcakes are brushed with brandy and apricot glaze to encourage the marzipan to adhere to the surface. Marzipan-covered cakes should rest for between one and seven days before being frosted.

Equipment
* cake board

Ingredients
* 8in (20cm) fruitcake
* apricot glaze
* confectioner's sugar

...apricot glaze encourages marzipan to adhere

COVERING WITH MARZIPAN

Carving and covering cakes **p.65**

Building tiered cakes **p.68**

Building with pillars **p.69**

Building asymmetrical cakes **pp.70–71**

1 Place the cake on a cake board. Use a pastry brush to cover it with apricot glaze (see Tip).

2 Roll out the marzipan into a circle 16in (40cm) in diameter and ½in (1cm) thick.

3 Lift it over the top of the cake so that it is centered and smooth it over the top, pushing out any air bubbles. Press the paste down around the sides. If it cracks, pinch it together or patch it with excess. Rub it with your fingers to smooth. Trim off any excess.

Chocolate

A versatile ingredient that you can use for many decorating techniques, chocolate can be temperamental. Whether you make ganache to frost cakes, melt and temper to create delicious decorations, or prepare a batch of chocolate clay (see pp.44–45), follow instructions carefully.

Making ganache

Ganache is simply chocolate melted into cream, which is then whisked to silky perfection. It can be poured over a cake while warm, or left to cool and spread with a palette knife (see opposite).

 PREP 5 mins

 COOK 5 mins

 MAKES 2 cups

Ingredients

* ¾ cup heavy cream
* 7oz (200g) good-quality dark, milk, or white chocolate, broken into pieces

Variations

For a sweeter flavor, try milk chocolate, but allow a longer time to set. You can chill ganache and make into truffles, beat into a fluffy frosting, or beat into buttercream for an even richer frosting. Make white chocolate ganache in the same way.

1 Break the chocolate into pieces and place it with the cream and chocolate in a medium heavy-bottomed pan and stir over low heat until the chocolate has melted.

2 Remove from the heat, transfer to a heatproof bowl, and whisk until glossy and thick. Pour over the cake or let cool for 1–2 hours before spreading.

Melted chocolate is the basis of a host of frostings, molded decorations, and other embellishments.

Tips

For a smooth ganache surface, dip a knife into hot water, dry with paper towels, and then run over the surface of the cake. You can use a knife or scraper to create textures. Try marbling with dark or white chocolate ganache.

Covering with ganache

Ganache is a popular alternative for those who find buttercream too sweet. It can be poured over chilled buttercream for a smooth layer, or spread onto a cake that has been leveled and filled.

 TIMING 20 mins

Equipment

* cake drum or board
* turntable or lazy Susan

Ingredients

* 2-layer cake, cooled and leveled (see p.29)
* 1 batch ganache (see opposite)

1 Place the base layer of the cake on the cake drum, set on a turntable. Spread a good quantity of soft ganache over the top with a palette knife. Place the next layer on top.

2 Drop a dollop of ganache over it, spreading it around. Apply a little more to the center and repeat, bringing it down the sides. Turn the cake as you hold the flat side of the palette knife against the ganache. Continue to spread until smooth (see p.31).

Melting and tempering chocolate

Whether you want to wrap a cake (see Variation, opposite), use molds to create decorations (see pp.120–23), or make curls or cigarillos, you must melt and temper chocolate so that it becomes hard and glossy. The recipe below makes enough to wrap a cake or to fill three large molds.

 PREP 5 mins, plus cooling

 COOK 10 mins

 MAKES 1lb 2oz (500g)

Equipment

* candy thermometer

Ingredients

* 1lb 2oz (500g) good-quality milk, dark, or white chocolate

...provide a hard, glossy finish

USING MELTED CHOCOLATE
Using chocolate molds **p.60**
Cutting chocolate shapes **p.61**
Piping with chocolate **p.85**

1 To melt the chocolate over a pan, break it into squares and place in a dry, heatproof bowl. Bring a pan of water to simmer.

2 Set the bowl over the pan. The bottom should not touch the water. Be sure there is no space between the bowl and the pan rim.

3 Stir occasionally to distribute the heat. Heat until the candy thermometer measures 113°F (45°C).

4 Remove from the heat and allow to cool until the temperature is 80°F (27°C), stirring frequently.

Melting and tempering in a microwave

This takes less time than the traditional method, but it may take some practice, since you will have far less control of the heat. As with the traditional method, it is best to use a specialized candy thermometer to test the temperature regularly. Overheating will cause the chocolate to take on a "white bloom" once hard.

 PREP 5 mins, plus cooling

 COOK 5 mins

 MAKES 1lb 2oz (500g)

Equipment
✳ candy thermometer

Ingredients
✳ 1lb 2oz (500g) good-quality milk, dark, or white chocolate

Variation
To wrap a frosted cake, spread tempered chocolate over acetate that is a little larger in size than the circumference and a little wider than the height of your cake. As the chocolate begins to harden, wrap it around the cake. When it is hard, remove the acetate.

1 Break the chocolate into squares, place it in a microwavable bowl, and heat on full power for 30 seconds. Stir, and heat again in 15-second bursts until the chocolate is smooth and melted.

2 Test the temperature and continue to heat in short bursts until it reaches 113°F (45°C). Allow to cool until the temperature is 80°F (27°C), stirring frequently. The chocolate should remain at this temperature as you use it, for instance, for wrapping a cake (see Variation). Warm it a little if it drops too low.

Making chocolate curls

You can make curls with chocolate that has just been melted, but more attractive results are achieved with tempered chocolate (see pp.40–41). Apply more or less pressure with your knife or scraper to vary the thickness. Scraping right through to the paper gives a full, steady curl.

 PREP 10 mins, plus cooling

 COOK 10 mins

 MAKES 12–24 curls

Equipment

* scraper or metal
  spatula, optional

Ingredients

* 7oz (200g) dark, white,
  or milk chocolate,
  melted and tempered
  (see pp.40–41)

Tips

For chocolate shavings, use a vegetable peeler to "peel" shavings from a square of chocolate in short, firm strokes. Use a cheese shaver for bigger shavings or curls. White and milk chocolate are softer and much easier to use than dark chocolate.

1 Spread the chocolate over parchment paper on a baking sheet. Tap the sheet to release air bubbles. Chill until just hard.

For small curls, use a knife to scrape the chocolate toward you, forming curls with the blade. If it is too hard, let it warm a little first.

For large curls, use a scraper to push the chocolate away from you, digging right through the surface.

2 Lift the curls with a skewer to keep from leaving smudges or melting the chocolate. Refrigerate until required.

Painting chocolate leaves

Create realistic foliage for molded or modeled chocolate flowers, or add a simple embellishment to cakes by painting melted chocolate over leaves straight from the garden. Choose fresh, nonpoisonous leaves, and wash and dry them before using.

 PREP 15 mins, plus cooling

 COOK 10 mins

 MAKES 12 large or 24 small leaves

Ingredients

* 7oz (200g) dark, white, or milk chocolate
* 12 large or 24 small, fresh, nonpoisonous leaves
* royal icing or edible glue, optional

Variation

For cigarillos, paint tempered chocolate over an acetate square. Leave ¼in (5mm) unpainted at an edge. Roll it, press the 2 painted edges together, and tape the unpainted edge to the outside. Cool. Freeze for 15 minutes, and slit the tape to reveal a cigarillo.

1 Melt and temper the chocolate (see pp.40–41). Dip a pastry brush in the chocolate and paint it over the back of a leaf. Place it on a plate or a sheet of parchment paper to cool and harden. Repeat with the other leaves. Apply more layers of chocolate for thicker leaves.

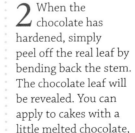

2 When the chocolate has hardened, simply peel off the real leaf by bending back the stem. The chocolate leaf will be revealed. You can apply to cakes with a little melted chocolate, a dab of royal icing, or some edible glue.

Chocolate clay

This malleable medium allows you to create sculptures, ribbons, swags, and figures with ease. Unlike tempered chocolate decorations, it dries firm and has no risk of melting. It is too firm to cover a cake with, but if you want to wrap a cake in chocolate, you could use flavored fondant (see p.46).

 PREP 15 mins, plus hardening   **COOK** 10 mins   **MAKES** 1lb (450g)

Ingredients

* 14oz (400g) dark, white, or milk chocolate
* ¾ cup corn syrup

Create decorative chocolate touches with ease

MODELING WITH CHOCOLATE

Modeling a rose **p.88**

Modeling a tulip **p.89**

Modeling a basic figure **p.92**

Modeling embellishments **p.96**

Using multi-ribbon cutters **p.118**

Using silicone molds **p.120**

1 Melt the chocolate in a large heatproof bowl over a pan of simmering water. In a small pan (or the microwave) heat the corn syrup until runny and warm. Pour into the melted chocolate. Remove from the heat.

2 Stir together until the chocolate and corn syrup form a ball and come away from the sides of the bowl. You may need to add more syrup, depending on the cocoa content of the chocolate. If it takes a long time to form into a ball, add a little more syrup.

3 Pour the ball onto some plastic wrap and wrap carefully. Leave for 2–3 hours to harden. Avoid getting water anywhere near the clay, since it will cause it to mark and separate—giving your decorations an imperfect finish.

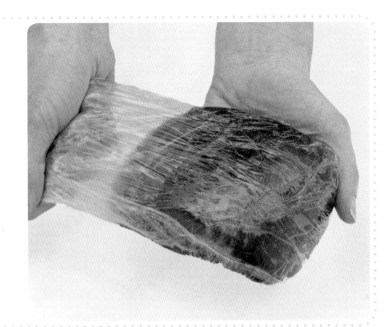

4 When it is hard, break some off and knead it with your hands until it is pliable. Use it to fill silicone molds (see p.120) or to model figures, flowers, swags, and other shapes. If the chocolate hardens, simply knead it again and the warmth of your hands will soften it.

Chocolate clay *is a great medium for modeling ribbons and bows (p.96).*

Fondant

Fondant, also known as sugarpaste, is a versatile product. Use it to cover cakes and drums, and to create stunning decorations. It can be colored, flavored, cut, embossed, and used in molds. If you do not want to make it, buy in any color from cake-decorating suppliers.

Traditional fondant

This is a classic recipe that works well for all types of fondant creations. It will keep for weeks if wrapped tightly and stored in an airtight container.

 PREP 20 mins

 MAKES 2lb 2oz (1kg)

Ingredients .

* 2 sheets gelatin
* ½ cup liquid glucose
* 1 tbsp glycerine
* 9 cups confectioner's sugar, plus extra for dusting
* coloring paste

Tips
Pure extracts, oils, pastes, or powders (such as vanilla, almond oil, or cocoa powder) can flavor fondant. Knead in 1–2 drops of flavoring at a time, distributing evenly. Allow the fondant to rest in an airtight container for 30 minutes.

1 Soak the gelatin sheets in a bowl of cold water for about 10 minutes. Wring dry and stir into ¼ cup warm water, one at a time, until dissolved. Mix in the glucose and glycerine until well blended, and set aside.

2 Sift the confectioner's sugar into a large mixing bowl. Create a well in the center and pour in the liquid a little at a time. Stir, and mix until it forms a soft ball.

One of the most versatile *ingredients, fondant can be used to cover cakes and create an array of decorations.*

Variation

Marshmallow fondant is more pliable than traditional fondant. Melt 10 cups mini marshmallows in a microwave until just melted. Stir in 9 cups confectioner's sugar until smooth. Add more if necessary. Turn onto a greased surface, and knead until smooth.

3 Dust a surface with confectioner's sugar and lay the ball of fondant onto it. Knead it with your fingers until it is smooth and pliable, adding a little water if it is dry, or a little confectioner's sugar if it becomes sticky. When it reaches the desired consistency, roll it out and use it immediately, wrapping any leftovers in plastic wrap for later use. Leave fondant-covered cakes to set and acquire a crust. Decorations eventually dry hard, but can take up to a few days, depending on the humidity in your environment.

4 To color the fondant, use a toothpick to apply a little coloring paste to the surface. Fold the fondant over the paste and then knead until it has a uniform color throughout. For a marbled look, mix 1 or more colors of paste into the fondant and knead it only partway through—creating a streaked effect. Marble just before you want to roll out the fondant. Kneading it again will cause the marbling to disappear.

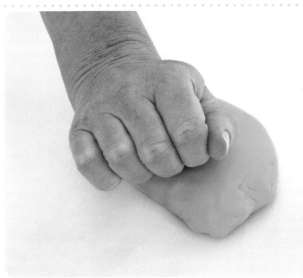

Fondant shapes *can be embossed with textured sheets and cutters (see pp.104–05).*

Using embossing mats

This is an easy way to imprint fondant with texture, whether you are embossing the whole surface of a cake or decorations. You could, for example, create a leather texture on a handbag cake. Some mats have holes in them, allowing you to paint the surface of the fondant through them (similar to a stencil).

Equipment
* fondant roller
* embossing mat

Ingredients
* confectioner's sugar
* 2lb 2oz (1kg) fondant
* vegetable shortening, for greasing
* cake, crumb-coated with buttercream frosting

...an easy way to imprint fondant with texture

EMBOSSING WITH MATS

Carving and covering cakes **p.65**

Building asymmetrical cakes **pp.70–71**

Painting a color wash **p.146**

1 Use confectioner's sugar to dust a surface. Lightly grease the fondant roller and roll out the fondant, to ¼in (5mm) thick.

2 Grease the embossing mat and place it greased-side down onto the fondant. Roll evenly over the top of the mat.

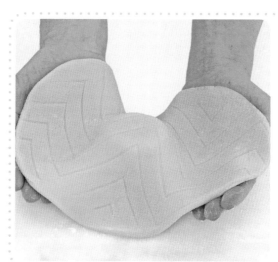

3 Remove the mat and lift the fondant over the top of the crumb-coated cake, using your hands to smooth it down gently without disrupting the pattern. You can also use this technique to emboss a covered cake drum (see p.51).

Using embossing rollers

There is a wide range of different textured rollers that provide detail to the surface of fondant. Delicate patterns like this damask-style roller can transform cake coverings. You can also purchase "sleeves" that slip onto fondant rollers and work in the same way.

Equipment

* ❋ fondant roller
* ❋ embossing roller

Ingredients

* ❋ confectioner's sugar
* ❋ 2lb 2oz (1kg) fondant
* ❋ vegetable shortening, for greasing

...provide detail to the surface of fondant

Tips

Buy embossing sticks to create patterns. They are ideal for smaller decorations or for cakes that are not fully embossed. Use vegetable shortening instead of confectioner's sugar or cornstarch—these can cause cracking when pressed into the fondant.

1 Follow step 1, opposite, but roll out the fondant so it is just a little thicker. Carefully and lightly grease the embossing roller. You can also dust it with cornstarch, but make sure to brush off any excess to keep from disrupting the fine detailed pattern.

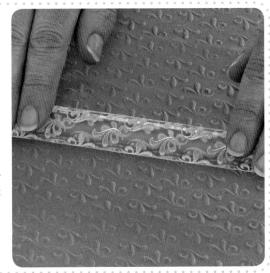

2 At the edge closest to you, press the roller into the fondant and push it away from you, all the way to the other side. If you have a sheet of fondant that is wider than the roller, line up the roller so that it overlaps with the section that has already been embossed by about ⅛in (3mm). Keep the roller straight as you roll, applying even pressure.

Covering a cake

Apply fondant to leveled, filled cakes that have been crumb-coated with buttercream or wrapped with marzipan. If you are covering a traditional fruitcake, brush the marzipan with a little water or brandy before you apply the fondant to ensure that it adheres. Smooth out the air bubbles as you cover the cake.

Equipment
* cake drum or board
* fondant roller
* fondant smoother

Ingredients
* confectioner's sugar
* 10in (23cm) 2-layer cake crumb-coated with buttercream (see p.29)
* 2lb 2oz (1kg) fondant

Smooth out the air bubbles as you cover the cake

Variation
Mini cakes are frosted in the same way as large cakes; however, the fondant should be thin—for large cakes, roll it to about ⅛–¼in (4–5mm) thick; for mini cakes, it should be ¹⁄₁₆–⅛in (2–3mm) thick. For cupcakes, cut out circles to sit on top.

1 Dust a surface with confectioner's sugar. Knead and roll the fondant into a circle 2in (5cm) wider than the cake.

2 Unroll the fondant sheet onto the cake and smooth it across the top with a smoother, easing it down with your hands.

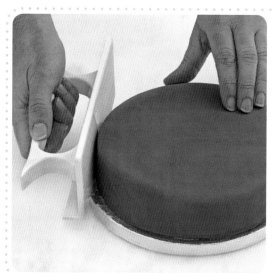

3 Trim off the excess fondant. Press the smoother evenly over the top of the cake and then run it down and around the sides of the cake until perfectly smooth. To get a sharp edge at the top of the cake, you could use 2 smoothers at the same time, 1 on the top and the other on the sides, pressing them together at the edge.

Covering a cake drum

Cover cake drums in fondant using matching or contrasting colors of your choice. You can emboss the fondant in the same way you would when covering a cake (see pp.48–49), add stripes or other detail, and even paint or dust it. Always let it set overnight to firm up before you decorate further.

Equipment

* cake drum
* fondant roller
* fondant smoother

Ingredients

* confectioner's sugar
* tylose powder
* 2lb 2oz (1kg) strengthened fondant (see p.87)

...emboss the drum in the same way you would a cake

Tip
To keep from damaging the surface of the covered drum, place the cake on a board the exact size of the cake. Add a dab of edible glue or water to the center of the board and place the cake on top. You can use ribbon or piping to mask the join.

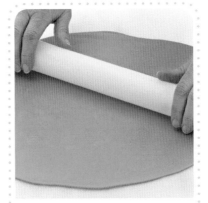

1 Dust confectioner's sugar on a surface and roll the fondant out into a circle ¹⁄₁₆in (2mm) thick and 12in (30cm) in diameter.

2 Mix together a pinch of tylose powder with 2 tablespoons of cold water until well blended and then brush over the cake drum.

3 Carefully lift the fondant onto the drum and, using a smoother, smooth from the center outward to remove air bubbles. Press down around the sides and trim off any excess around the bottom of the drum with a sharp knife. Glue an edible or fabric ribbon around the circumference to finish.

Gum paste

Although traditionally used for fragile flowers, gum paste can be used to make any decorations you wish. It dries very hard, and, even though it is technically edible, it is not normally eaten. You can color it in the same way as you would with fondant.

 PREP 30 mins, plus thickening and chilling

 MAKES 1lb 2oz (500g)

Ingredients

* 2 tsp powdered gelatin, dissolved in 5 tsp warm water and allowed to thicken for 30 minutes
* 2 tsp vegetable shortening
* 2 tsp liquid glucose
* 4 cups confectioner's sugar, sifted, plus extra for dusting
* 4 tsp tylose powder
* 1 large egg white
* coloring paste, optional

Tips

Keep gum paste in an airtight container until ready to use. If the paste is sticky, work in a little more vegetable shortening until smooth and pliable. If it is too hard and crumbly, add a little more beaten egg white.

1 Place the thickened gelatin in a pan with the vegetable shortening and glucose. Stir over low heat until the liquid is clear.

2 Transfer to the electric mixer bowl, adding the confectioner's sugar, tylose powder, and egg white. Mix at the highest setting.

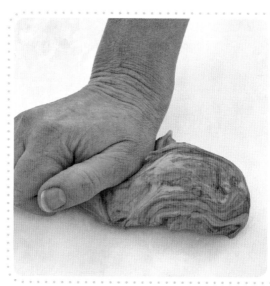

3 Continute to mix until stringy and white. Refrigerate the mixture for 24–48 hours. Dust a board with confectioner's sugar and knead the mixture until smooth and pliable. Color the paste, as shown with fondant on p.47.

Mexican paste

This soft paste is ideal for cutting out shapes and modeling, since it does not stretch or lose its shape. Mexican paste is often used with tappits and patchwork cutters (see pp.116–17). It takes a little time to incorporate the confectioner's sugar, but its firm results are well worth the effort.

 PREP 30 mins, plus chilling

 MAKES 7oz (200g)

Ingredients

* 1⅔ cups confectioner's sugar, sifted, plus extra for dusting
* 3 tsp tylose powder
* vegetable shortening, for greasing, optional
* coloring paste, optional

Tip
Avoid using cornstarch to dust surfaces when preparing pastes, since it will make the paste harder. Once the paste is ready, you can use cornstarch to dust in the usual way, although vegetable shortening does produce better results with pastes.

1 Stir the confectioner's sugar and tylose powder in a bowl. Add 2 tablespoons of cold water and stir until the mixture holds well.

2 Place on a surface dusted with confectioner's sugar. Knead until you have a smooth ball. Do not add any more water.

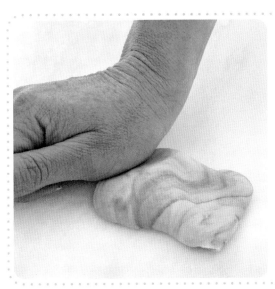

3 Wrap in plastic wrap and chill for 24 hours. Remove from the refrigerator and knead on a surface dusted with confectioner's sugar or greased with shortening until smooth and pliable. Color it now, or spray, paint, or dust it when decorations are dry.

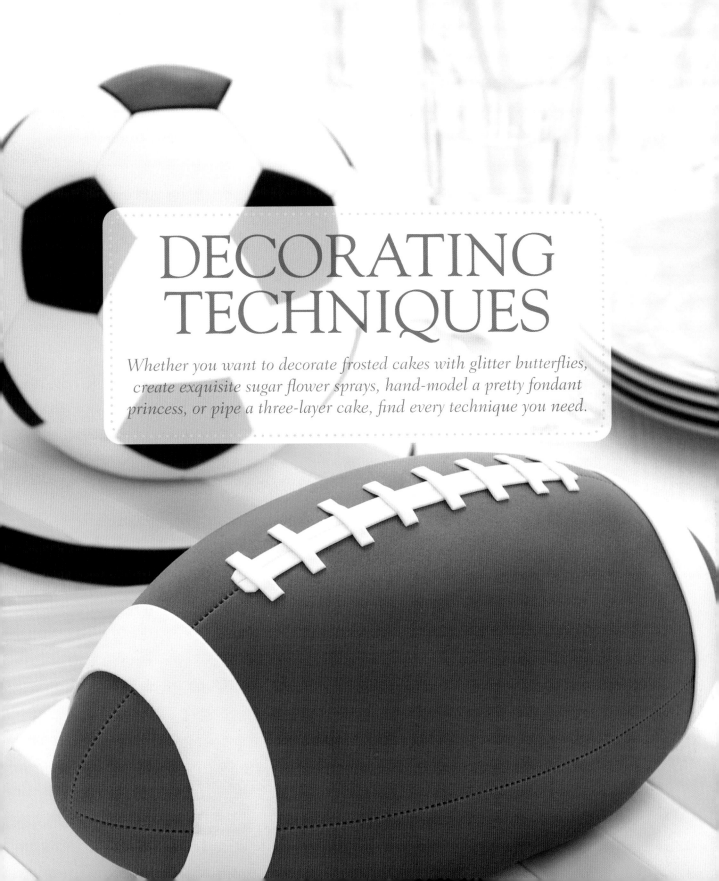

DECORATING TECHNIQUES

Whether you want to decorate frosted cakes with glitter butterflies, create exquisite sugar flower sprays, hand-model a pretty fondant princess, or pipe a three-layer cake, find every technique you need.

3-D CREATIONS

*Make your cakes truly spectacular and build strong
foundations for your designs by using 3-D decorating techniques
and a little imagination. Find out how to carve a cake into
a novelty shape; create a model from rice treats; build durable
shapes with gingerbread, fondant, or chocolate; and
stack cakes into tiers with dowels and pillars.*

Making a template

Templates are important when building easy and accurate 3-D shapes. Draw around them to cut out the pieces of fondant, chocolate, or modeling paste that you need. You could draw on graph paper first, to help you with the proportions, or trace directly onto parchment paper.

Equipment

* graph paper
* cardboard

Create accurate and easy 3-D shapes by tracing your own templates

1 Trace the outline of a shape you want to duplicate, such as a shopping bag, onto graph paper. Neaten the outline, using a ruler to make it symmetrical, if necessary. When you're happy with it, transfer it onto parchment paper and cut it out. Dust it with cornstarch to prevent it from sticking to your medium.

2 To ensure that the template is accurate, cut the shapes from cardboard and glue them together as a trial run. You can also use this sample to support your creation as it dries.

Tip

Use hand-drawn or traced templates to sculpt slabs of cake into shapes, such as flowers with curved petals, Christmas trees, cartoon characters, or animals. Once you have a good outline, use the small leftover chunks of cake as fillers for the shapes.

Using crisp rice shapes

Use crisp rice cereal to create decorative 3-D designs. These are pliable and hold their shape well, allowing you to make intricate designs, which are often not possible with cake. For best results, refer to the object or a photograph of the object you are recreating.

Ingredients

* ✱ 4 tbsp unsalted butter, softened
* ✱ 3 cups miniature marshmallows
* ✱ ½ tsp pure vanilla extract
* ✱ 5 cups crisp rice cereal
* ✱ confectioner's sugar, for dusting
* ✱ buttercream frosting (see pp.24–25)
* ✱ sheet of fondant, rolled to ¼in (5mm) thick

1 Melt the butter in a large pan over medium heat and add the marshmallows. Cook for 3 minutes, stirring, until the marshmallows melt. Stir in the vanilla extract, remove from the heat, and add the cereal, mixing everything together. Transfer to a bowl and refrigerate until firm, about 1 hour.

Variation

You can use food-safe plastic, resin, rubber, or silicone molds to create detailed shapes. Dust with a little cornstarch or confectioner's sugar, and then press the mixture firmly into the mold. Refrigerate until firm, ease out, and cover with fondant (step 6).

2 Using a sharp knife, carve the basic shape of the model, and then work on finer details. If necessary, you can soften the crisp rice mixture any time by heating it for a few seconds in the microwave. This will make it more pliable, especially for molding the smaller details.

3 You can also dust your hands with confectioner's sugar, warm the mixture slightly in your hands, and then mold it into shape. The firmer it is pressed, the more likely it is to hold its shape. Use cutters, if needed.

4 Mold details such as teddy bear ears, limbs, and other small parts with your hands and press them onto the model. If you need to, use toothpicks to keep them in place.

5 When the model is complete, refrigerate until firm (at least 1 hour). Gently warm a little buttercream frosting to soften it, and brush over the model. This will help to fix the fondant in place.

6 Fold the fondant over the figure, pressing down gently. If you like, add pieces of fondant over the base layer to create details, moistening the back of each piece with water to make the fondant adhere.

Using chocolate molds

Build 3-D chocolate creations using large plastic molds. There are several types of mold, such as this piano, that allow you to assemble an entire 3-D construction. Use dark, milk, or chocolate, so long as it is correctly tempered (see pp.40–41).

Equipment
* ✳ mold
* ✳ soft cotton gloves

Ingredients
* ✳ dark or white chocolate, melted and tempered (see pp.40–41)

1 Polish the mold by wiping it with dry cotton balls. Lay it on a baking sheet on a flat surface, propping up all the parts evenly.

2 Spoon the chocolate into the mold, and press it into the crevices with the back of a spoon. Tap it gently to release air bubbles.

Tips
Place the chocolate creation on top of a cake, or to its side, and keep in a cool room until ready to display. If there are any marks on the chocolate, spray it evenly with confectioner's glaze to produce a more uniform and shiny appearance.

3 Refrigerate the chocolate for about 20 minutes, until set. Gently tap the mold to release the pieces onto parchment paper.

4 Wearing gloves, trim off any excess with a knife. Brush melted chocolate onto the pieces to join them. Allow to harden.

Cutting chocolate shapes

Use a template or hand-drawn pattern to cut shapes from a slab of hardened chocolate and assemble a 3-D construction, such as sides for a box. Use a very sharp, warm knife that cuts through the chocolate neatly, and work fast, since chocolate can melt quickly when handled.

Equipment
* food-grade acetate sheets
* cardboard or baking parchment templates

Ingredients
* dark or white chocolate, melted and tempered (see pp.40–41)

...cut shapes from a slab of hardened chocolate

Variation
You can create curved 3-D surfaces by placing another acetate sheet on top of the chocolate slab. When it begins to harden but is still pliable, carefully wrap it around a bowl or can. This will help to support its weight and create a curved shape.

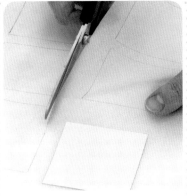

1 Line a baking sheet with a food-grade acetate sheet. Cut out templates (see p.57) from parchment paper.

2 Spread the melted, tempered chocolate over the acetate with a palette knife to the desired thickness. Chill for 15 minutes.

3 Trace the templates with a knife, cutting through most of the surface. Return to the refrigerator and chill until hard.

4 Heat a sharp knife in hot water, wipe dry, and cut through to the base of the shapes. Assemble as described opposite.

Building with fondant

Create buildings, bricks, and other 3-D shapes like this boat, by using fondant stiffened with tylose powder, tragacanth gum, or gum paste. Mold fondant to form any shape and join the pieces together using edible glue. Use a template to design a unique 3-D decoration.

Equipment

* cardboard or parchment paper templates
* cardboard or cardboard box, for supports

Ingredients

* cornstarch, for dusting
* strengthened fondant (see p.87)
* edible glue

Mold fondant to form any shape you like

Tip

For tall creations, insert a cake-pop stick, a wooden skewer, or a food-safe wire into the fondant to provide support. Strengthened fondant dries out quickly, so work on small portions at a time, keeping the remainder covered in plastic wrap.

1 Dust a surface with cornstarch and roll out the fondant to the desired thickness. Roll it thickly if it needs to support other parts.

2 Cut the desired shape using a template (see p.57) or a ruler. Then, cut a base to support the creation.

3 Dry for 2–3 days on parchment paper, until firm. For arched shapes, place pieces on a curved, cornstarch-dusted surface.

4 Pipe, paint, or draw details onto dry shapes before you join them, making sure not to smudge them as you do so.

5 Using a small, clean paintbrush, join the shapes together with edible glue, or by simply moistening the sides with water and holding them firmly in place until they stick.

Variation

Press the strengthened fondant into molds (such as building blocks or other shapes; see pp.120–23) and, once dry, stack or layer them to create a 3-D construction. Work carefully with delicate creations, since they can break easily.

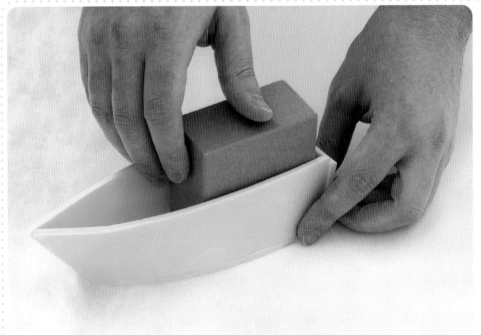

6 It is a good idea to provide some support inside the creation until the glue dries. Fold a small cardboard box to support a design such as this boat. You can place a box or a cylinder inside a fondant building or a turret to give added support.

Creating strong 3-D objects

For complex modeling paste objects, such as this shoe, use cardboard or paper templates to ensure accuracy. Choose a sturdy paste, such as gum or Mexican paste, and provide adequate support for the shapes as they dry, so that they maintain their 3-D quality.

Equipment

* cardboard or parchment paper templates
* cardboard box, for support

Ingredients

* sheet of gum paste, or other modeling paste
* cornstarch, for dusting
* edible glue

1 To make a shoe, roll the paste on a cornstarch-dusted surface. Roll a thick piece for the sole. Use a knife to cut around the template.

2 Create a support for the shape. For a high-heeled shoe, use a cardboard box covered in plastic wrap for support.

3 Make supports for each part, and let dry overnight. When nearly dry, check the shape and adjust, if needed.

4 To form the shoe, paint edible glue on the edges and press them together. Allow each part to dry before moving on to the next.

Tip

While the paste is still slightly pliable, emboss the surface with modeling tools or cutters, pressed just into the paste but not through it. This is a good way to make a shoe label, for instance. Decorate after the glue has fully dried.

Carving and covering cakes

Carve cakes to create 3-D replicas of almost anything, from handbags and trains, to cars and guitars (see below). Choose a firm, dense cake such as pound, which will hold its shape and support the weight of the frosting. Be sure the cake has cooled before you freeze it.

Equipment
* cardboard or parchment paper templates

Ingredients
* buttercream frosting (see pp.24–25)
* round or square pound cake, depending on the shape of your design (see p.231)
* sheet of fondant, rolled to ¼in (5mm) thick

Tip
Every carved cake needs a basic layer of fondant wrapped around it, as shown in step 3. Once this has rested and formed a crust, you can add more layers of fondant in different colors, as well as detail and other decorations.

1 Spread buttercream frosting between the layers of your cake, and freeze for 30 minutes. For tall designs, thin layers work best.

2 Use a very sharp knife to carve the cake into the basic shape you want. Then use a small, sharp knife for detailing.

3 Let the cake rest for an hour. Crumb-coat with buttercream frosting (see p.29), then cover with fondant. Press it into the crevices.

For 2-D shapes, use a very sharp knife to cut carefully around a template. Neaten the edges and then proceed with step 3.

Building with gingerbread

The secret to a successful gingerbread construction is good-quality dough, a symmetrically drawn template, and precise baking time. You will also need patience, since you have to wait for the glue or royal icing fixative to dry as you construct, to ensure a sturdy finished product.

Equipment

* cardboard or parchment paper templates

Ingredients

* gingerbread dough (see p.235), rolled to ¼in (5mm) thick
* royal icing, for piping (see pp.34–35)

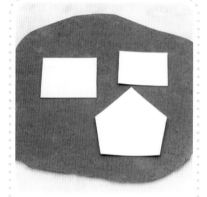

1 To create a house, lay the templates on the gingerbread dough. Use a sharp knife to cut around the templates neatly.

2 Using a palette knife, move the dough pieces onto a baking sheet lined with parchment paper, making sure they lie flat.

Variations

You can create trees, towers, windmills, and fairy canopies with gingerbread. For cylindrical shapes, wrap the gingerbread pieces around a can while they are warm. If you are worried whether the construction will work, do a trial run with cardboard and glue.

3 Bake according to the recipe instructions. Trim any rough edges with a sharp, hot knife, and let the pieces cool.

4 Once cool, pipe your designs on the cooled gingerbread pieces before you assemble your creation, if desired.

5 To assemble, work from the bottom upward, applying royal icing to the seams with a palette knife.

6 Allow each seam to dry. Be sure the base is dry before you attach the roof. Hold the pitched roof in place for a few minutes.

Once dry, pipe the roof with royal icing to create snow and icicles, or simply decorate to taste

Use thin layers of icing to stick the pieces together, allowing each layer to dry before adding another

Tips
Always assemble the gingerbread construction on the board on which it will be presented. Moving it later could cause pieces to shift. Royal icing can be colored with shades of coloring paste, helping to make the piping stand out.

Building tiered cakes

Stack a light, frosted sponge cake directly onto the cake below it without support. For dense cakes covered in fondant or any cake structure taller than two layers (as shown here), you will need dowels and cake boards to keep the structure steady and prevent it from collapsing.

Equipment

* cake boards, in varying sizes, to suit size of cakes
* dowels
* wire cutters

Ingredients

* fondant-covered or smooth-frosted cakes in varying sizes, according to your design
* confectioner's sugar
* royal icing, for sticking

Variation

Use a long dowel and embed it through all the cake tiers from top to bottom. This will keep the structure steady and prevent movement. Cut circles from the center of each board in advance, to make it easier for the dowel to run through.

1 Dust the bottom cake with confectioner's sugar. Put a board the same size as the small cake on top. Press down gently for a guide.

2 Insert a dowel into the cake. Nick it with a knife at the height of the cake. Cut all dowels to the same height with wire cutters.

3 Insert the dowels into the cake straight down, until they touch the board. Space them 1in (2.5cm) in from the guideline.

4 Carefully center and then attach the small cake and its board on top with a little royal icing. Repeat for more tiers.

Building with pillars

If you want to use solid pillars, simply dowel the cake (see opposite), positioning the dowels where you want the pillars to be. Place the pillars on top of the dowels, securing them to the cake and to the cake board above, with royal icing. For hollow pillars, follow this step-by-step.

Equipment

* dowels
* 6 pillars
* wire cutters
* cake boards, in varying sizes, to suit size of cakes
* piping bag with small, round tip, optional

Ingredients

* fondant-covered or smooth-frosted cakes in varying sizes, according to your design
* confectioner's sugar
* royal icing, for sticking

Tip

An easy and reliable way to construct a tiered cake is to use a specialized stand—cakes sit on plates that fit directly into it. You can also use interlocking separators that fit over a central post, thus perfectly centering the tiers and supporting them.

1 Place the dowels where you want the pillars to sit—evenly spaced around the cake. Mark the cake with the position of each.

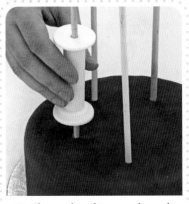

2 Place a dowel into each mark, pushing it through the cake until it hits the board beneath. Slide the pillar over the top.

3 Using wire cutters, cut the dowel so it is the exact height of the top of the pillar. Cut the other dowels to the same height.

4 Pipe or spread royal icing to the top and base of each pillar, slide them onto the dowels, and place the cake and board on top.

Building asymmetrical cakes

Asymmetrical cakes are not only visually stunning but are also relatively easy to make, so long as you use a firm, dense cake (such as pound cake) and a dowel in the center for support. Begin by partially freezing each cake on its board, since this makes carving easier.

Equipment

* 1 cake board, for the base
* 2 or more cake boards, the size of your cake tiers, with a hole the width of the dowel pierced through their center
* long wooden dowel, sharpened at one end
* shorter dowels (see p.68)
* wire cutters

Ingredients

* 2 or more pound cakes (see p.231), in varying sizes, according to your design; levelled and layered with buttercream
* buttercream frosting (see pp.24–25)
* cornstarch, for dusting
* fondant

1 Carve the cakes when they are almost frozen. Carve the top of the base tier at an angle so it slopes at a diagonal level.

2 Position the next tier on top. Hold it firmly with one hand, and use a knife to score the top of the cake at an opposite diagonal.

3 Check that the layers are even. Repeat to add more tiers. Use the tier beneath for support as you cut.

4 When the cakes are all cut with angled tops, crumb-coat each cake (see p.29) and chill for 30 minutes–1 hour.

5 Dust a surface with cornstarch and roll out a large piece of fondant. Carefully lift it over the top of the bottom tier, smoothing downward to cover it (see p.50). Repeat with all the tiers, until each one is fully covered.

6 To stack the cakes, insert dowels (see p.68) in all the tiers except the top one. Cut each dowel using wire cutters to make sure that it sits flush with the top of each angled cake.

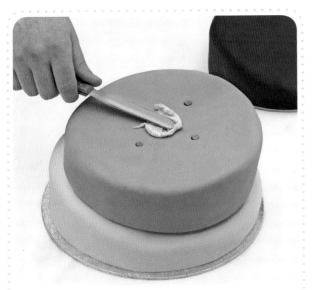

7 Dot buttercream frosting in the middle of each tier and stack one on top of the other, making sure they are centered. The long dowel should run smoothly through the cakes and the holes in their boards.

8 Carefully press the long dowel through all the tiers until it hits the cake board of the base tier. Cut it so that it is exactly the same height as the uppermost tier. Add a decoration to disguise it.

PIPING

Master the art of piping and elevate your cakes from simple to sensational. Start by learning how to make and fill a piping bag and practice the techniques—soon you'll be creating intricate piping with ease. Pipe flowers, foliage, borders, lettering, embroidery, beading, stringwork, and other decorative touches using a variety of piping tips and ingredients.

Making a piping bag

Make a piping bag yourself using a square of parchment paper. Fill it with a small quantity of your piping medium, and pipe fine lines and effects easily. Snip the end and pipe without a tip, or add a tip of your choice (see p.20), with or without a coupler.

Equipment

* parchment paper or tracing paper
* masking tape

Simply snip the end and pipe with small quantities of icing

1 Fold the lower corner of the parchment paper upward so that it is folded in half diagonally. Run your finger along the fold.

2 Fold over the whole of the top folded section without creasing it, rolling it over until you have a cone shape.

3 Fold the bottom folded section around the outside. Using your hand, expand it out, and then secure with a little masking tape. Cut off any excess paper from the top.

Tip

Large piping bags are also known as "pastry bags," although they can be used for any type of piping work. Be careful not to overfill the bags, even when piping large quantities of icing, since this makes it difficult to apply uniform pressure.

Filling a piping bag

A piping bag should be densely packed with filling, but only at the tip end—don't overfill it. Squeeze the icing toward the tip, removing any air bubbles. Use any one of the huge variety of tips available to create a multitude of decorative touches on cakes and cupcakes.

Equipment

* ✳ piping bag with tips
* ✳ coupler, optional
* ✳ scraper, optional

Ingredients

* ✳ colored royal icing, for piping (see pp.34–35)

Squeeze the icing toward the tip, removing any air bubbles

Tip

Couplers are devices that allow you to change tips without emptying or refilling the piping bag. A base piece is placed inside the bottom of the bag, a tip is fitted into the screw-on top, and the top and tip are then screwed onto the base.

1 Fit the tip to the piping bag, with a coupler, if desired, and place it upright in a tall glass. Spoon in the icing.

2 Remove the bag from the glass and lay it on a flat surface. Squeeze the icing toward the tip, using a scraper, if desired.

3 Lift up the piping bag and twist the excess bag at the top to make sure that the icing is tightly wrapped. Pipe as usual (see opposite).

Basic royal icing piping

Learn how to apply pressure to the piping bag correctly and increase your piping confidence. Create small or large decorative touches by controlling the flow with firm or light pressure. Stop the pressure completely and lift the tip away at the end of each design.

Equipment

* piping bag with tip

Ingredients

* royal icing, for piping (see p.35)
* cake, fondant-covered or iced with royal icing

Control the flow with firm or light pressure

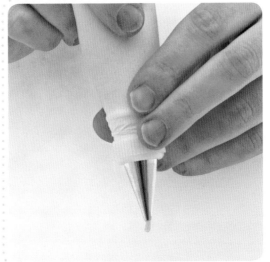

1 Fill the piping bag with royal icing, as shown opposite. Hold the bag in your right hand (or left, if you are left-handed), between your thumb and first 2 fingers. Hold the bag steady with your other hand. When the tip touches the surface of the cake, gently squeeze out the icing.

Tip

The consistency of icing is very important. Make sure the royal icing is firm, but not runny. If it is too hard, the lines will break, curl, or crumble; too soft, and they will run. See p.35 for details about royal icing for piping.

2 Even pressure is crucial. Too little pressure will produce scrawny lines, while too much will make the process difficult to control. Let the icing catch the surface and gently lift the tip away from the surface, letting the icing fall. At the end of the line, stop the pressure and lift the tip.

Piping with buttercream frosting

Much softer than royal icing, buttercream can be piped with any tip and in any color to create a wide variety of decorative effects on frosted cakes or cake drums. It's perfect for cupcakes, too. Varying the size of the tip and the pressure you apply can change the design dramatically.

Shell border

Use a medium open star tip for a shell border. Allow the frosting to fan out as you drag and drop.

Zigzag border

An open star tip can create an attractive pattern that works well on the surface of cakes.

Swirl border

Use an open star tip to create a series of interlinked, scroll-like swirls.

Dot border

Create a row of symmetrical dots or beads with a medium round tip.

Stars and star border

Create individual stars (below) or link them together as a border, using a medium open-star tip.

Piped leaves

Use a small leaf tip to create leaves, ruffling the lengths and dragging the frosting to a tip.

Basket weave

A medium basket-weave tip is used here, with small sections of piping in a woven pattern over longer lines of buttercream.

Grass

Short strands of grass (and even fur or hair) can be created with a small multi-opening grass tip.

Longer grass

Pipe longer, wider strands of buttercream with a medium multi-opening grass tip to create grass and individual hair strands.

Rosette border

Use a medium open star tip to swirl tiny rosettes that can be linked or used individually.

Pulled bead border

Use a medium round tip to pipe beads and then slowly release the pressure as you drag each bead.

C-scroll border

Linking up a series of "C"s, using a small open-star tip, creates an easy and pretty border; alternate "C"s with "S"s for a different look.

Rope border

Create a sturdy rope or a series of scrolls by linking a series of backward "S"s with a medium open-star tip.

Ruffle border

Pipe a simple ruffled border using a medium petal tip, dragging the frosting back on itself and then forward again.

Piping buttercream borders

Buttercream is an excellent medium for piping decorative borders and effects. You can pipe figures, flowers, and other decorations, and even use it for brushwork embroidery (see p.139). Get the consistency of the buttercream right (see p.24) and use the correct tips.

Equipment
* piping bag equipped with an open star tip (such as Wilton no. 21), filled with buttercream frosting (see pp.24–25)

Ingredients
* smooth-frosted cake on a fondant-covered cake drum

Buttercream is excellent for piping borders and effects

Tip
If the buttercream has air bubbles after beating, press them out against the sides of the bowl with a spatula to help you achieve a smooth product. Don't overfill the bag, since it will warm in your hands and the frosting will melt.

1 For a shell border, hold the bag at a 45° angle just above the cake surface. Squeeze, so that the frosting fans out.

2 Relax the pressure and pull the bag along the bottom of the cake. Pull the tip along to form a point. Repeat.

For drop flowers, hold the bag directly above the cake surface, just touching. Squeeze, letting the frosting build up to make a flower. Stop squeezing then lift the tip away. You can turn the hand that is holding the bag as you squeeze out the frosting for a swirl, and/or add a dragée to the center.

Piping a buttercream rose

Pipe a simple rose using buttercream frosting. It can be piped onto a small square of parchment paper, directly onto a cake in a single movement (see Variation), or piped onto a flower nail, as shown here, and then applied to the cake once the buttercream has firmed a little.

Equipment

* piping bag, equipped with a coupler and a round tip (such as Wilton no. 12), filled with buttercream frosting (see pp.24–25)
* petal tip (such as Wilton no. 104)
* flower nail

1 Hold the tip above the center of the flower nail. Apply pressure and squeeze out a cone shape of frosting.

2 Change to a petal tip. Hold the bag at a 45° angle and squeeze to form a ribbon of frosting that overlaps at the top of the cone.

Variation

To pipe a buttercream rose with a single movement, attach a large or medium open star tip to your piping bag. Pipe a dab of buttercream to create a center, and then carefully work your way around the center in a counterclockwise motion to create a swirl.

3 Place the wide end of the tip against the base of the bud. Squeeze and move the tip up and then down to the base. Repeat for 3 petals around the bud, overlapping each petal just behind the edge of the first. Repeat the same technique, creating a row of 5 petals and, finally, a row of 7, angling the tip to create an open rose.

Piping dots, beads, and flowers

Decorate the top of a cupcake with a series of simple, piped royal-icing picot dots, beads, and flowers. Picot is a type of elegant "embroidery" that can be undertaken with a series of small, simply piped dots. For a different effect that is as easy to achieve, try a beaded border.

Equipment

* piping bag fitted with a small, round tip (such as Wilton no. 1L), filled with piping-consistency royal icing (see p.35)

Ingredients

* cake, fondant-covered or iced with royal icing

For picot dots, hold the bag so the tip is just above the cake. Pipe a dot, increasing pressure to increase its size. Stop squeezing to drop it.

For beads, hold the bag at a 45° angle. Apply pressure as you lift to allow the icing to spread out. Stop the pressure as you drop it.

Tip

When piping picot dots, do not gradually stop the pressure or you will get a "nose" on the dot. Instead, stop squeezing and pull away immediately. Allow to dry just slightly, dip your finger in a little cornstarch, and gently press it down.

For flowers, prepare the bag as before. Pipe a small dot and then push the point of the tip into the edge and drag it toward you in a petal shape. Continue, piping another dot beside the first one, working in a circle, until you form a flower.

Piping filigree with royal icing

Using a series of interlinked "W"s and "M"s, or simply long, continuous curls and lines, filigree is an elegant piping technique that you can use to create delicate, lacelike designs. Similar in approach, scrolled hearts can be piped on parchment paper and attached to the cake once dry.

Equipment

* piping bag fitted with small, very fine round tip (such as PME 00 or 0), filled with piping-consistency royal icing (see p.35)
* template, optional

Ingredients

* cake or cupcake, fondant-covered or iced with royal icing
* edible glue

1 Pipe an outline with the tip positioned just above the surface of the cupcake. Apply uniform, gentle pressure.

2 Pipe curves, bending continuously in all directions, but never touching. Do not lift the tip from the surface.

Tips

For more intricate designs, you can use an icing "pen," which you fill with icing and use with one hand. The pen pushes the icing out without the need to squeeze. You can also purchase icing syringes, which require special tips.

For scrolled hearts, use a template, if desired, to pipe a design onto a sheet of parchment paper. Dry until hard (overnight, if possible), carefully remove from the parchment, and affix the hearts around the sides of your cake with a little edible glue.

Piping with royal icing

Create elegant and detailed designs with royal icing, which can dry hard and hold its shape for 2-D and 3-D work. Color as desired and use with different tips for varied effects. Piping is a skill really worth mastering, to achieve a truly professional finish.

Scrolls
Use a small shell or rope tip to create a series of interlinked scrolls for a border on a cake.

Rope
Use a rope tip to pipe a spring shape in a clockwise direction, using even pressure.

Filigree
This delicate piping work is created with a small writing tip and long piped lines of random patterns. Dust with luster dust to highlight.

Beads and stringwork
Try small and large writing tips to create a finely piped line of beads. Link with loops of piped string work.

Shells and stringwork
Use a shell tip to create a row of symmetrical shapes and then link them with piped stringwork, finishing off with a picot dot at the base of each shell.

Ruffles and rosettes
A star tip creates a lovely rosette when turned in a clockwise motion. Link with a series of ruffles, using a small petal or open star tip, and embellish with stringwork.

Shell border with stringwork

Use a shell tip to create a continuous shell border, and then a writing nozzle to pipe in diagonal lines for a lattice beneath.

Star border

Create a star border in any size, with an open star tip. Apply pressure until you get the required size, and then lift the bag upright for each shape.

Pulled beadwork

Use a slightly larger writing tip to create soft beads of icing and then drag them across to form a thinner tail.

Skein border

A skein is created with a small star tip by piping in a clockwise direction at an even height to form the first curve and then pulling down in a point.

Zigzag ruffles

Use a small open star tip and pipe in a delicate back-and-forth motion to create the appearance of ruffles.

Swirls and picot dots

Use a fine writing tip to create elegantly piped curls, surrounding the larger swirls with a series of picot dots.

Damask 1

This ornate design can be created using a fine writing nozzle to pipe over a template or in the cutout sections of a stencil.

Damask 2

To create this delicate pattern on the side of a cake, press a template onto the surface of the fondant and use a veining tool to emboss the shape for piping.

Trailing branches

Create fine and then slightly wider lines with a fine writing tip. Use the same tip for the beaded blossoms on the branches.

Piping lettering

Piped lettering is one of the trickiest skills to learn, but if you master the technique you will be able to add a professional touch to your cake. The secret of successful piping is patience and practice. Pipe on parchment paper, then freeze until hard, or pipe directly onto your cake.

Equipment

* tracing paper or parchment paper template
* piping bag with small, round decorating tip (Wilton no. 1L)

Ingredients

* royal icing, for piping (see p.34) or thinned buttercream (see p.24)
* cake, fondant-covered or iced with royal icing

Tips

Use royal icing to pipe onto fondant-covered cakes and use buttercream frosting for buttercream-frosted cakes. Use more pressure for heavier lines (downstrokes, when writing in script) and less for thinner lines (upstrokes).

1 Place your template (if using) on the cake and use a toothpick to mark out the letters. Fill the piping bag with icing.

2 Place the tip just above the surface of the cake, with the bag at a 45° angle, and begin piping.

3 Apply pressure and drag the tip along the surface as you form the letters. Release the pressure to end a line.

For block letters, apply pressure, lift, and move along the line of the letter. Release pressure with the tip pressed onto the surface.

Piping with chocolate

You can pipe chocolate onto the surface of a cake, or you can let the designs harden in the fridge on a sheet of parchment paper, ready to affix later. Chocolate should be lukewarm to pipe effectively. Temper the chocolate (see pp.40–41) for the shiniest, hardest results.

Equipment
* tracing paper or parchment paper template
* piping bag with small, round decorating tip (such as Wilton no. 1L)

Ingredients
* milk, white, or dark chocolate, melted and tempered (see pp.40–41)

1 Fill the piping bag with melted and tempered milk chocolate that has cooled slightly, so it is just warm. Fix a sheet of parchment paper on top of the template, and secure the sides with paper clips to hold it steady.

Tips
You can also pipe directly onto a cake, as you would with royal icing or buttercream frosting. You may, however, find it easier to pipe onto a chocolate or fondant plaque, because you can wipe off the piping and start again if you make a mistake.

2 Press the tip against the surface of the parchment paper at the center of the design and, working from the inside out, pipe lines over the template. Drag the tip along the paper, leaving a neat line of piping. Stop the pressure at the end of each line, and repeat, piping each line separately. Chill until hard.

HAND-MODELING

Work malleable mediums such as fondant and gum paste by hand to produce beautiful decorations that enhance your cakes. Make delightful 3-D models, such as realistic flowers and leaves, or characters for novelty cakes, with the help of the right tools and these impressive techniques.

Strengthening fondant

Whether you choose to model fondant entirely by hand, or you use cutters to create a variety of shapes, it is important to prepare the fondant so that it is pliable, strong, and able to dry hard enough. Use small quantities at a time, leaving the rest double-wrapped in plastic wrap.

Ingredients

* ✳ vegetable shortening, for greasing
* ✳ 1lb 2oz (500g) fondant
* ✳ 2 tsp tylose powder

...pliable, strong, and able to dry hard enough for cutting and modeling

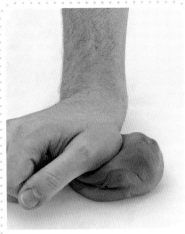

1 Lightly grease a flat surface and place the fondant on top. Knead the fondant until it is smooth. Make a well in the center.

2 Place the tylose powder inside. Press the fondant around the well and knead the ingredients together.

3 When the fondant is smooth, pliable, and evenly colored (with no streaks of strengthening powder), double-wrap it in plastic wrap and place in a zippered bag for 1–2 hours, or overnight. You can omit this resting time, but the fondant will lose some elasticity.

Tips

Always use "flower" grade or finely milled tylose powder to strengthen fondant. Coarser-milled powders are fine for making edible glue, but will make fondant lumpy and cause it to harden unevenly. Strengthen after coloring fondant, not before.

Modeling a fondant rose

You can easily mold impressive, blooming roses using your fingers and a ball tool, as shown here. To save time and create an even shape, you could cut out the petals using petal cutters in a mix of three or four sizes. This technique works well with chocolate clay, too.

Equipment

* 18-gauge floral wire
* ball tool

Ingredients

* 1oz (25g) fondant, strengthened (see p.87)
* vegetable shortening, for greasing

Mold impressive, blooming roses

Tips
Knead in a little more tylose powder or tragacanth gum when modeling the cones, so that they require less drying time. It is possible to create a rose on an undried cone, but it may not hold its shape as successfully.

1 Form a cone of fondant on the wire. Place upright to harden for 3 days. When dry, grease your surface and roll a ball of fondant.

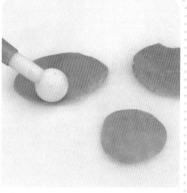

2 Press out into a small oval, ¹⁄₁₆in (1mm) thick. Create 5 more and cover with plastic wrap. Use a ball tool to soften the edges.

3 Moisten the base of each petal with a little water and attach to the cone, overlapping each petal to form a tight bud.

4 Repeat, molding larger petals. Add around 20 petals, using larger petals to form an open rose. Place on a stand to dry overnight.

Modeling a simple tulip

Tulips are easy to make and, unlike roses, require only one cutter. Use a calyx cutter for the base, or form a star with your fingers. Alternatively, you could hand-model the petals as you would for the rose (see opposite), with one end of the oval slightly narrower than the other.

Equipment

* fondant roller
* petal cutter
* scriber tool
* calyx cutter

Ingredients

* vegetable shortening, for greasing
* 1oz (25g) fondant, strengthened (see p.87), rolled to ⅟₁₆in (2mm) thick
* ½oz (12g) green fondant, strengthened (see p.87)

Variations

To create frilled petals for the tulip, make tiny cuts around the petal outline, then roll a frilling tool over the edge of each petal. To make your own inedible stamens, use thick thread that has been stiffened with edible glue, attaching a small ball of fondant at the tip.

1 On a greased surface, roll a tiny ball of fondant. Cut out 3 petals using the cutter. Draw down the center of each, using a scriber tool.

2 Moisten the base of a petal, and press it around the ball. Repeat with all petals. Overlap them for an open tulip.

3 Roll out the green fondant, and cut a calyx with the cutter. Moisten and press onto the base of the tulip. If desired, you can press the petals closed at the tops with your fingers.

Creating flowers and sprays

Cut and vein realistic flowers from fondant or gum paste, tint them with petal dust, and then wire them together for dramatic sprays (see pp.112–13). There is a wealth of cutters that can produce many types of flower. They provide the perfect finishing touch to any celebration cake.

Poinsettia

Cut out petals and leaves in a range of sizes, vein them with a veining mat, and layer to create a gorgeous Christmas blossom.

Purple roses

Wire simple fondant roses in vibrant colors into sprays for dramatic effect.

Orchids, cornflowers, and baby's breath

Create a trailing spray by wiring together larger flowers at one end and smaller ones at the other, filling spaces with blossoms and leaves.

Calla spray

A simple spray of uniform-sized lilies is easy to wire with veined green foliage and it makes a stunning and effective centerpiece.

Orchid spray

Wire together an orchid, cut from thinly rolled paste and tinted dust, with foliage and tinted blossoms. Use a sharp knife to vein the leaves.

Freesia

Tint fondant or paste to a pale lilac and create a spray of freesia, wrapping the blooms together with floral tape (see p.112–13).

Cornflowers

Use specialized cutters for vivid blue cornflowers. Using a garlic press, create strands of paste that can be rolled into shape for the central stamens.

Cymbidium orchid

Stipple the inside of the flower's bell with a stiff brush and a little petal dust mixed with grain alcohol. Ruffle the veined bell with a frilling tool.

Gerbera and freesia

A daisy or gerbera plunger cutter will emboss the surface of the petals. Layer and wire with freesia and blossoms.

Jasmine

Try using a calyx cutter for jasmine. Lightly tint the centers of jasmine blossoms with pink petal dust to highlight the veining on the petals.

Freesia trailing spray

Wiring together single leaves on a central wire creates a trailing spray. Bright freesia with white stamens are accompanied by individually wired white blossoms.

Lilies

Wrap teardrops of white paste around sturdy yellow stamens. Score the leaves and petals for realism.

Rose spray

Use a little brown petal dust on gum-paste leaves, and then steam to provide a soft sheen. Attach to rose buds in various sizes.

Orchid

Create the petals and center of an orchid with a specialty cutter and a veining tool. Try using darker petal dust on the outside edges, softening the shade toward the center.

Modeling a basic figure

With some careful modeling and sculpting, you can make figures like this little girl. You can use a veining tool to add creases to fabric, or a frilling tool to form curls in the strands of fondant hair, if desired. You can even adapt her to become a princess (see pp.170–75).

Equipment

* cake-pop stick, halved
* stitching (quilting) tool
* veining tool
* scalpel
* toothpick
* fondant roller
* small blossom cutter
* garlic press

Ingredients

* 3½oz (100g) each of lilac and pale pink fondant, strengthened (see p.87)
* 1oz (50g) flesh-colored fondant, strengthened (see p.87)
* black edible pen
* pink edible pen
* pink luster dust
* cornstarch, for dusting
* 1 tsp yellow fondant, strengthened (see p.87)
* 1oz (25g) brown fondant, strengthened
* edible glue

1 Form a large ball of kneaded fondant into a teardrop shape. Flatten the top and base, and smooth it down so that the base fans out. Insert the cake-pop stick through the center. Shape a smaller ball of lilac fondant into a bodice shape. Slip it onto the stick and add detail with a stitching tool. Use a veining tool to score folds.

2 Model 2 narrow cones of pale pink fondant that are curved at each end, with one end wider than the other. Use the veining tool to score creases into the sleeves, and bend the arms at the elbow. Allow to harden for 30 minutes, and then moisten with a little water and attach to the top of the bodice.

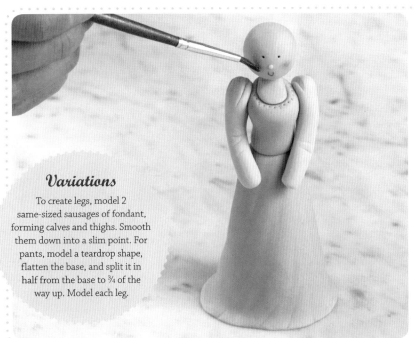

Variations

To create legs, model 2 same-sized sausages of fondant, forming calves and thighs. Smooth them down into a slim point. For pants, model a teardrop shape, flatten the base, and split it in half from the base to ¾ of the way up. Model each leg.

3 Knead the flesh-colored fondant into a neat oval that fits into the neckline of the dress, moisten the base and slide it onto the stick. Smooth it down into the bodice and use your fingers to create the neck. Allow to dry for 30 minutes while you make the head. Form an egg-shaped ball of flesh fondant into a head, with a gentle curve for the chin and a tiny oval for the nose. Mark the eyes with the fine black edible pen and draw in the mouth with the pink pen. Brush the cheeks with a little pink luster dust and slide the head onto the stick.

4 Cut a thin strip of pink fondant and attach it to the waist. Cut 2 more strips and fix to the front of the skirt for a sash. Create hands by shaping flesh-colored fondant into 2 tiny teardrops. Use a scalpel to cut 4 fingers and a thumb on each hand, and then add shape using a toothpick. Poke a small hole into the wrist of each arm and attach the hands to the sleeves. Draw one over the other and secure with a little water. Roll out the strengthened yellow fondant on a cornstarch-dusted surface and cut a blossom with the cutter. Fix it to the bodice. Press balls of brown fondant through a garlic press to create hair. Glue the strands onto the head with edible glue so that the sections meet at a side parting.

Modeling characters

Color and model strengthened fondant, modeling pastes, or clays to create delightful characters for your cakes. You can embellish them with the use of basic tools, piping, edible paints, dusts, and pens... and a little imagination.

Ballerina
Use a garlic press to make natural-looking hair and a frilling tool to create the skirt. Paint the laces for the ballet shoes.

Ladybug
Use a large round piping tip to cut black fondant dots and flower stamens for the antennae.

Mouse
You can pipe or purchase googly eyes, then score a thin rectangle of gum paste for the teeth.

Rabbit
Create the body in a single color and add the features afterward, scoring the cheeks with a frilling tool.

Fairy
Rice paper, cut to shape, makes delicate wings. Try marbling the base of the toadstool.

Cat
Flower stamens make great whiskers. Scoring the fondant creates the furry stripes.

Dog
Try using veining and frilling tools and pieces of fondant to add detail to the face and body.

Chicken
Fondant wings can be scored into feathers with the back of a knife.

Elf
Give his clothing a realistic touch by pleating the fondant and scoring in folds with a veining tool.

Sheep

A frilling tool creates fluffy white-fondant fleece. Let the fondant dry before adding the black details.

Baby ladybug

Use a circle of thin white gum paste or rice paper for the eyes. Color in the pupils with a black edible pen.

Pirate

Use stitching and veining tools to emboss the clothing and give his beard a realistic touch.

Cow

This cow has modeled legs on a basic tear-shaped body. The spots are shaped individually.

Dragonfly

Carefully score a fondant body with a thin knife or scalpel and adorn with rice-paper wings.

Teddy bear

Use a blade or stitching tool to add seams, then pipe a dot of black icing onto thin fondant circles for his eyes.

Pig

A basic tear shape can form the body of a pig, or any number of different creatures.

Elephant

It is all in the detail! Gently scored lines produce a lovely weathered hide. Model the trunk and head in one piece and then add ears.

Soccer player

Make your player's body first and then "dress him" with thinly rolled fondant shapes.

Westie

Create his fur with a veining tool and by simply pulling bits of the fondant into points.

Modeling embellishments

You can adorn cakes or decorations with swags, bows, ruffles, ropes, and chains. These techniques take a little time to master, but they add beautiful detail to your creations. For prettier bows, use a stitching tool to quilt the edges of the swags before you pleat them.

Equipment

* ✳ fondant roller
* ✳ veining tool
* ✳ circular cutters,
    1 large and 1 small
* ✳ flower mat or foam
* ✳ frilling tool

Ingredients

* ✳ strengthened fondant
    (see p.87)
* ✳ cornstarch, for dusting

Add beautiful detail to your creations

Tips

Paint your chains (see opposite) with metallic luster dust mixed with grain alcohol one side at a time, allowing the paint to dry fully before turning over and painting the other side. You can also airbrush the links to create texture.

1 **For a swag**, roll out a small rectangle of fondant on a cornstarch-dusted surface, cut to neaten the edges, and pleat folds.

2 Gather up the fondant on each side, and pinch it together at the top, moistening it with a little water. Cut off any excess.

1 **For a bow**, create 2 swags. Fold them over so the pinched edges meet. Model a smaller rectangular swag for the center.

2 Attach with water. Wrap the center swag around the seam and fix together at the back. Use a veining tool to neaten the pleats.

1 **For ruffles**, roll out a thin square of fondant on a dusted surface and use a cutter to cut out a large circle. Use a small circular cutter to create a hoop, and cut through to create a strip. Transfer to a flower mat.

2 With the outside edge of the strip sitting on the edge of the mat, roll the frilling tool back and forth, pressing and stretching the fondant. Rotate the strip. To attach, moisten the reverse side with water.

For ropes, roll out the fondant on a dusted surface and cut into strips. Roll with your hands to create strands. Moisten the length of one and fix another to each end. Twist each end in the opposite direction.

For chains, cut untwisted ropes into even-sized pieces. Make a link by moistening the ends of one piece of rope with water and pressing them together to make a neat seam. Repeat, looping each link as you go.

Modeling with marzipan

You can sculpt, smooth, and reshape marzipan as much as you wish, since it is soft and pliable and takes a long time to dry. Marzipan fruits are traditionally used to decorate Christmas fruitcakes. They are pretty, easy to make, and can be created with very little equipment.

Equipment

* veining tool, optional

Ingredients

* cornstarch, for dusting
* 7oz (200g) marzipan (see p.36)
* 1 tsp tylose powder, optional
* red, brown, and green coloring pastes
* edible glue

Tip

To make edible glue, mix ¼ teaspoon of finely milled tylose powder with 2 tablespoons of warm water. Mix together until most of the lumps have dissolved. Cover and refrigerate overnight. When it is ready, it will have a syrupy consistency.

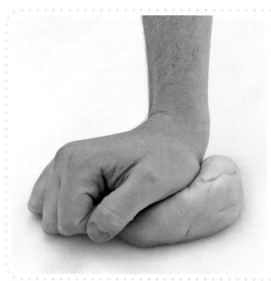

1 Dust a flat surface with cornstarch and warm a little marzipan in your hands. Knead it until it is soft and pliable. If you need the decorations to harden more quickly, knead in a little tylose powder (see p.87).

2 Break 2 golf ball-sized pieces of marzipan from the ball and set aside. Use a toothpick to dab red coloring paste into the center of the rest and knead until evenly distributed. Add more paste until you get the desired color. Color one of the golf balls with brown paste and the other with green in the same way.

3 Take a ball of red marzipan and form it into a soft, smooth cone. Press each "strawberry" all over with the end of a toothpick, to make seedlike impressions. Poke a hole in the top for the stem.

4 Use the same technique to make the apples, creating slightly rounder cones with a flatter base. Use a veining tool to poke a hole in the center of each apple.

5 Use green marzipan to form leaves and stems. Take a tiny flat, oval piece and then mold until you have the desired shape. Green and brown stems can be made by rolling the marzipan into a narrow rope.

6 Attach the stems to the pieces of fruit using edible glue. Glue one leaf on each side of the brown stem for the apples, and a crown of leaves around the strawberry stems. Allow to harden for about 24 hours.

USING CUTTERS AND MOLDS

An incredible variety of cutters and molds makes it easy to achieve a professional finish. They are fuss-free and require very little experience to use. These techniques show you how to use them, providing you with the specialized guidance you need to create perfect fondant stars, butterflies, and lacework ribbons.

Using plunger cutters

Plunger cutters provide detailed decorative shapes with minimal effort. Use cutters with fondant, gum paste, Mexican paste, and chocolate clay, and try experimenting with layers, shapes, and painted effects to produce a unique array of finished decorations.

Equipment
* fondant roller
* plunger cutters
* forming tray, optional
* flower mat or foam, optional
* ball tool, optional
* dowel or roller, optional

Ingredients
* cornstarch, for dusting
* fondant, or any other modeling paste or clay
* tylose powder, to strengthen fondant, (see p.87), optional

...detailed decorative shapes with minimal effort

1 Dust a surface with cornstarch. Knead the fondant, adding tylose powder for firmer shapes. Roll it out to the desired thickness.

2 Dust the cutters with cornstarch. Holding the cutter at the base, press down into the fondant and lift out.

3 With the fondant in the cutter, rub the edges to remove uneven bits. If the cutter does not have embossing, move to step 5.

4 Place the cutter on a surface and press the plunger down firmly. This will emboss designs onto the surface of the shape.

TECHNIQUE CONTINUES · · · ·

5 Lift the cutter up so it is just above the surface, and press the plunger again to release your shape. If you are using an embossing cutter, it should now be embossed with the design. These embossed marks are useful when you come to paint or dust decorations.

6 Gently transfer the shapes onto a flower mat or foam. Use a ball tool to shape them and add definition, if desired.

Tip

If the fondant or gum paste sticks to your cutter, dust the cutter with cornstarch or lightly grease with vegetable shortening and try again. It can also help to let the fondant dry out for a few minutes before recutting the shape.

7 You can release shapes into forming trays to dry in a natural shape for at least 3 hours. Curl shapes around a dowel or roller to give them a natural curve.

Variations

Use cutters to cut out shapes from a sheet of fondant. Where the gaps are left, fill with shapes from another shade of fondant. You can easily remove the plunger and transform the cutter into a basic plaque cutter (see pp.106–07).

For more delicate shapes, roll the fondant very thin and allow it to dry for up to 30 minutes, forming a light crust, before cutting. This helps to ensure easy release from the cutter and a clean, even shape. When the shapes are intricate, like this snowflake, run a sharp knife around the edges and into the grooves of the cutter to release any trapped fondant and create a crisp edge.

Plunger cutter designs

Available in a wide range of shapes and sizes, plunger cutters make cutting simple and embossed shapes easier than ever to make. They also create quick, accomplished decorations with a perfect finish. Layer, paint, and shape your designs to achieve a unique look.

Butterflies

This cutter embosses with detail. Dry in the crease of an open book to keep the wings upright, or dust with glitter to highlight.

Daisies

Cut out a basic daisy shape with the marguerite daisy cutter. If you don't press down on the plunger when you are cutting, your flowers will be unembossed.

Blossoms

Cut blossoms in a variety of shapes. The ball in the cutter embosses a circular center that can be topped with a bead of royal icing or fondant, and also curls the petals upward.

Hearts

A heart plunger cutter creates uniform shapes that can be painted or sprinkled with glitter for dramatic effect.

Stars

Star plunger cutters come in many sizes and produce crisp, perfectly formed edges. These simple stars are ideal as cake or cupcake toppers.

Circles

Circle plunger cutters will become one of the mainstays of your cake-decorating toolkit, and you can use them to cut flawless circles in a variety of sizes.

Gerbera

Use a marguerite daisy cutter in a variety of sizes to produce a beautiful, layered gerbera. Make indents in the center with a toothpick for authentic detail.

Layered stars

Layering multicolored shapes in different sizes produces pretty decorations to match your color theme. Glue them by moistening the backs with water.

Embossed blossoms

Cutting the outline of a blossom rather than embossing the center produces a good basic shape that can be embossed and dusted.

Embossed hearts

Cut hearts from embossed fondant or gum paste, or run an embossing roller over the surface of the hearts after cutting. Always emboss while the fondant is still soft.

Glitter stars

Cut stars from embossed fondant and sprinkle with glitter or luster dust to produce a pretty shimmer.

Layered flowers

Simple, unembossed daisies form the basis of these decorations. Letting them dry a little before layering helps them to keep their shape.

Using cookie cutters

Use traditional plastic or metal cookie cutters to cut gum paste or fondant into a variety of shapes, such as these hearts and stars. You need to remove the paste from this kind of cookie cutter yourself, while plunger cutters do this for you. Allow the shapes to dry before painting.

Equipment

* fondant roller
* cookie cutters
* veining, embossing or ball tools, optional
* flower mat or foam, optional

Ingredients

* cornstarch, for dusting
* gum paste, other modeling paste, or fondant (strengthened, if desired; see p.87), rolled to the desired thickness
* edible glue, optional

...create a variety of shapes, such as these hearts and stars

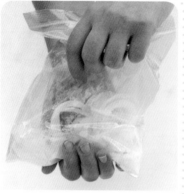

1 Put some cornstarch in a plastic bag with the cookie cutters. Shake to coat them, then remove and lightly tap to remove excess.

2 Press the cutters into the paste, cutting all the way through. Move the cutter from side to side to release the shapes.

3 Lift the cutter. If the paste sticks to it, use a veining tool to push it gently away from the edges. Moisten with water or edible glue and attach to your cake now, if desired, or move onto parchment paper to dry overnight.

All shapes should be dried and dusted to remove any excess paste or cornstarch before painting

Use a palette knife to transfer the decoration carefully to another surface for drying or shaping

5 Use veining or embossing tools to add detail (see p.110). Use a ball tool to shape and thin the edges of petals or leaves.

4 If you want to transfer them to another surface, such as a flower mat, use a palette knife to move them.

6 To use shapes for modeling, such as petals for a rose, loosely cover them in plastic wrap so that they remain pliable.

Mosaic and layering work

Layer different fondant shapes to create textured and multicolored decorations. Use small plunger cutters of the same shape to cut tiles, strips, or other shapes, and then join them together for a mosaic effect on a fondant decoration or the surface of a cake.

Equipment

* ✳ fondant roller
* ✳ cutters
* ✳ ball tool, optional
* ✳ flower mat or foam, optional

Ingredients

* ✳ fondant, or any modeling paste or clay
* ✳ cornstarch, for dusting
* ✳ edible glue, optional

1 **For a mosaic tile effect**, roll out the fondant to the desired thickness on a surface dusted with cornstarch.

2 Cut equally sized squares from the fondant. Moisten with edible glue or water, then paste onto a cake.

Tip
You can cut out pieces from the shapes you have layered on the top so that the base color or colors beneath show through. This is a particularly good method for creating windows on houses, buses, and cars.

For inlay patterns, cut out shapes, such as these polka dots, from a flat sheet of fondant. Then cut the same shapes again from a contrasting color of fondant, and insert these into the first fondant sheet. Gently roll to join and then use to cover your cake or create patterned decorations.

1 **For layered patterns**, such as flowers, place the largest flower shape at the base. Brush the center with edible glue or water, then place a smaller one on top. Continue with the remaining shapes.

2 You could transfer each shape to a flower mat and use a ball tool to model the petals after you have completed the layering. Let set before using edible glue or water to fix to your cake.

For multicolored, layered decorations, such as cars, teddy bears, or faces, cut out various elements of the design in the appropriate colors, using a template if necessary. Moisten the back of each element with a little edible glue or water, and continue layering until all the elements are in place.

Layer daisies *in bright colors (see pp.104–05).*

Embossing leaves and flowers

Shape and emboss to create realistic leaves and flowers, using one of many embossing and veining mats available. Ball, flower, and leaf tools add shape and definition. Many plunger cutters have veins and other features embedded, so they can do two jobs at once.

Equipment

* ❋ veining mat or sheet
* ❋ cutting wheel tool, optional
* ❋ flower mat or foam
* ❋ ball tool
* ❋ flower and leaf tool
* ❋ cone tool
* ❋ flower former, optional

Ingredients

* ❋ cornstarch, for dusting
* ❋ gum paste, modeling paste, or strengthened fondant (see p.87)
* ❋ vegetable shortening, for greasing

Variation

A veiner can be used to emboss ridges and impressions for leaf shapes. Place the shape on the veiner and use the ball tool or your fingers to press it down onto the mat. Turn it over, and continue with step 3, to enhance the shape.

1 For leaves, press rolled-out paste over a cornstarch-dusted veining mat pushing it into all the grooves and ridges.

2 Lift the paste off the mat and turn it over on the dusted surface. Use a cutting wheel tool or a knife to cut the outside edge.

3 Grease the surface of the tools with vegetable shortening, to prevent sticking. Transfer the leaf to the flower mat or foam, using a palette knife, and use the tools to enhance the grooves and ridges. Soften the edges to provide more shape. Leave on the mat to dry and harden overnight, if desired.

1 **For flowers**, dust a surface with cornstarch and roll out the paste. Cut out the flowers and leaves and transfer them to a sheet of parchment paper or a flower mat, using a palette knife.

2 To shape the flowers, use the ball tool to press down onto the edges of the petals. Gently move the tool toward the center of the flower to encourage the petals to form into cups.

3 Use the flower and leaf tool to score veins into the petals, to give them a realistic, textured appearance. To hollow out the center of the flower, press the cone tool into the middle of the shape. This is a good way to make holes through which wire and stamens can later be added. Leave on the mat, or transfer to a flower former, to dry overnight.

Creating flower sprays

All you need to create realistic sprays—displays of cascading flowers and leaves—are a few simple tools. Sprays can be informal tumbles or traditional bouquets, depending on the celebration. Wire them individually and then group them together on top of a cake.

Equipment

* 22- or 24-gauge floral wire
* wire cutters
* needle-nose pliers
* floral tape
* flower and leaf tool
* floral foam or Styrofoam, to keep flowers upright
* veining mat or mold
* ball tool, optional

Ingredients

* gum-paste or fondant flowers and leaves
* sheet of gum paste or strengthened fondant (see p.87)
* edible glue

1 Cut a length of floral wire, then bend the tip into a loop with needle-nose pliers. Wrap the loop with floral tape.

2 Form the paste into a small cone and press the loop into the center. Press down a flat end. Dab with edible glue.

3 Press the flower onto the flat surface. Hold for a minute to allow it to adhere. Place in floral foam or a piece of Styrofoam.

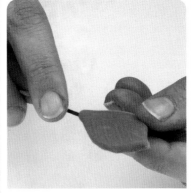

Variations

Wire hand-modeled flowers, such as roses, as you make them (see p.88). Flowers with holes in the center help with wiring—moisten the loop wire and press it onto the flower center. Moisten the center with edible glue or water and then feed the wire through.

4 Use a cutter or veining mat to cut out leaves thick enough for a wire to be inserted. Thin the edges with a ball tool.

5 A veining mat creates a useful ridge in the center of leaves. Slip wire into the ridge and tape it while the paste is soft.

Wrap each flower stem individually

One by one, add more flowers and leaves to the flower spray

6 Once dry, wrap together the wires of a leaf or two with floral tape, then attach to the base of one of the flowers.

Pull the floral tape up around the joins of the wire and press firmly to adhere

Embossing a patchwork design

You can use patchwork cutters to emboss the surface of a fondant-covered cake beautifully, or to create an interesting plaque. Emboss other decorative pieces that can then be painted, piped, or used as the basis for layered decorations on a cake or structure.

Equipment

* ✳ fondant roller
* ✳ patchwork cutters
* ✳ luster dust or spray, optional
* ✳ edible paint or felt-tip pen, optional

Ingredients

* ✳ vegetable shortening, for greasing
* ✳ fondant-covered cake or rolled fondant

Emboss decorative pieces that can be painted, piped, or used for layered decorations

To emboss a cake surface, lightly grease the patchwork cutters with some shortening and emboss all or part of a fondant-covered cake. Press the cutters firmly into the surface of the fondant. You can highlight or paint the impressions with luster dust or spray (see p.136).

To emboss a plaque, or any other decoration using rolled fondant, cut it to the desired shape, then press the cutter into the surface. Place it on parchment paper to dry. You can pipe around the design or use edible paint or edible felt-tip pens to highlight the impressions (see p.137).

Cutting a patchwork design

Use patchwork cutters to cut out a variety of shapes from gum paste, Mexican paste, or fondant and fix onto cakes. Very thin decorations are easier to cut, but will dry out more quickly. Push the cutter into the paste with a firm pressure and lift it out gently.

Equipment
* fondant roller
* patchwork cutter

Ingredients
* vegetable shortening, for greasing
* gum paste, other modeling paste, or strengthened fondant (see p.87)
* edible glue

Tip
An easy way to release the design from the patchwork cutter is to press the paste gently with your finger from the back. You can also use a veiner or the end of a toothpick to detach the paste gently from the intricate edges.

1 Lightly grease a flat, nonstick surface and the patchwork cutter with shortening. Roll out the paste to the desired thickness.

2 Press the entire outline of the cutter firmly to cut through the paste and then lightly press the central sections to emboss it.

3 Remove any excess paste, with the cutter in place. Use a palette knife to lift the shape onto parchment paper to dry.

4 Fix decorations to the surface of a cake, or let dry overnight and place decorations upright on it, brushing with edible glue.

Making a patchwork design

Build up a patchwork design to add detail and create an almost 3-D effect. You can build the design directly on the cake or on a piece of parchment paper, allowing it to dry and placing it flat or upright on the finished cake. Always start with the largest section of the design.

Equipment
* patchwork cutters
* fondant roller

Ingredients
* vegetable shortening, for greasing
* gum paste, modeling paste, or strengthened fondant (see p.87)
* edible glue

...add detail and create an almost 3-D effect

1 Lightly grease a patchwork cutter with shortening, and apply directly into a gum paste plaque, leaving an impression.

2 Store the pastes in plastic bags to keep them pliable. Choose colors for each section, then roll them out thinly.

3 Cut out the largest piece of the design. Position it on the embossed design and trim or press into shape as necessary.

4 Working with one color at a time, cut and affix all the pieces into place over the main design until it is complete.

Using tappits

Tappits are similar to patchwork cutters, but they come in strips that are pressed down into lengths of rolled fondant or paste, pressed through to cut, and then tapped out. Use them for creating delicate decorations or even neat numbers, letters, and other small shapes.

Equipment

* fondant roller
* tappit set, with rectangle cutter
* foam, optional

Ingredients

* vegetable shortening, for greasing
* sheet of strengthened fondant (see p.87), or modeling paste
* petal dust, optional
* edible glue

Tip

To release the cut designs from the tappits, tap them firmly against the corner of a hard surface before laying them on foam or parchment paper to dry. If they have lost their shape, adjust gently with your fingers or a veining tool.

1 Lightly grease the fondant and tappits. Place the strip cutter on the fondant and press down to cut. Remove excess fondant.

2 Place the tappit across the strip horizontally to cut one shape at a time. Press firmly so the edges cut all the way through.

3 Use a sharp knife to remove excess fondant. Use a palette knife to lift onto parchment paper or foam to dry until firm.

4 If desired, you can dust or paint the designs with petal dust before sticking them to your cake with edible glue.

Using multi-ribbon cutters

You can roll multi-ribbon cutters over the top of a sheet of paste or fondant to cut and emboss ribbons of all shapes and sizes. Decorate your cakes with ribbons or use them to create a variety of different stripes, bows, and swags.

Equipment

* fondant roller
* multi-ribbon-cutter set

Ingredients

* sheet of fondant (strengthened, if desired; see p.87), gum paste, or other modeling paste
* cornstarch, for dusting

...different stripes, bows, and swags to decorate cakes

Tips

Change the look of the ribbons by ruffling the edges (see p.97). Allow to set for a moment or two before applying to your cake, so they hold their shape, but don't wait too long or the fondant may crack.

1 Assemble the roller, using spacers to make the ribbons the desired width and the cutting wheels to produce the impression you want. Use wavy, beaded, or zigzag cutters for a variety of styles. Add spacers and tighten the bolt so that the wheels move backward and forward, instead of from side to side.

2 Place the fondant on a surface dusted with cornstarch. Press the ribbon cutter into the fondant at the edge closest to you, and press down on the roller so that it cuts through the fondant to the surface beneath. Continuing to press hard, roll the cutter away from you firmly, but gently. Repeat and trim excess with a sharp knife.

Using flat ribbon cutters

Flat ribbon cutters work like patchwork cutters or tappits, cutting the outside edges while embossing the surface. They can produce embossed, flat, frilled, ribbed, or scalloped ribbons. There are two ways to use these types of cutters, both of which result in flawless ribbons.

Equipment

* flat ribbon cutter
* fondant roller

Ingredients

* sheet of fondant (strengthened, if desired; see p.87), or modeling paste, cut into ribbon-width lengths

Create frilled, ribbed, or scalloped ribbons

Variations

Apply ribbons to your cake by moistening their reverse side with water or edible glue. You could wrap them around supports and dry them overnight, to create twists, bows, and other shapes. Apply these designs to your cake once they are dry.

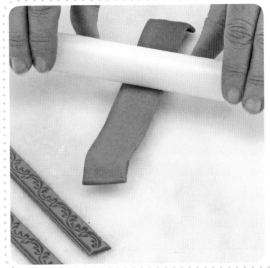

To lay the fondant on the cutter, place the cutter flat on a surface, with the cutting edges facing upward. Gently lift the fondant on top, to cover the surface, and use the roller to press the fondant into the cutting edges. Remove any excess, turn the cutter over, and tap to release the ribbons.

To lay the cutter on the fondant, place the cutter into the fondant or paste, and use the fondant roller to press it firmly into the surface, working from one end of the cutter to the other. Gently pull the cutter away from the paste to release the ribbons.

Using silicone molds

Use these pliable molds to create everything from attractive cupcake and miniature cake toppers to decorative elements for a whole cake. It is crucial to grease or dust molds well, so that you can remove the fondant shapes in one piece and with minimal effort.

Equipment

* silicone molds

Ingredients

* vegetable shortening, for greasing
* cornstarch, for dusting
* fondant (strengthened, if desired; see p.87), gum paste, or modeling paste

Variation

You can use different colors of fondant in a single mold, pressing small amounts of each color into the detail. Use a single base color to fill the mold to the top and join all the pieces together. Continue with steps 3 and 4.

1 Grease a clean silicone mold with vegetable shortening or dust it with cornstarch. Make sure to reach all the crevices.

2 Knead the fondant into a soft, pliable ball. Press the ball into the mold, using your thumb so that it fills the mold completely.

3 Cut off any excess and dry for a few minutes. If the fondant is not strengthened, place it in the freezer for a few minutes.

4 Bend the mold so the shape falls out. Trim the edges and moisten the back with water to apply to the cake, or allow to dry.

Using plastic molds

Plastic molds, like those used for chocolate molding (see p.60), are ideal for producing 3-D designs and decorations. If you are using a deep or wide mold, remember to allow plenty of time for the fondant shape to dry so that it holds its shape.

Equipment

* large plastic mold

Ingredients

* cornstarch, for dusting
* gum paste, or other modeling paste, or strengthened fondant (see p.87)

...ideal for producing 3-D designs and decorations

Tip

To paint the decoration, wait until it is just dry to the touch—it doesn't need to be completely dry, so test it after about an hour. Use a clean, dry brush to dust away excess cornstarch, and blot with a paper towel to remove any grease before you paint.

1 Brush the mold well with cornstarch and remove any excess. Knead the gum paste into a soft, pliable ball.

2 Press the ball into the mold, applying firm pressure with your thumb to ensure that all the details are filled.

3 Trim any excess from around the mold with a sharp knife. Freeze for up to 30 minutes, or until the paste is firm.

4 Tap the mold, then twist the opposite corners slightly so the shape falls out, flat side down. Dry on parchment paper.

Using resin molds

Resin molds often come with a piece of silicone in their center, which you can use to press paste deep into the mold and also to cut the edges. Resin molds are particularly useful for creating lacework (as below), scallops, borders, beading, and decorative embellishments.

Equipment

* ✳ resin mold with silicone insert
* ✳ fondant roller
* ✳ ball tool
* ✳ wire brush
* ✳ straight pin

Ingredients

* ✳ cornstarch, for dusting
* ✳ Mexican paste, strengthened fondant (see p.87), or other modeling paste
* ✳ petal dust, optional
* ✳ edible glue, optional

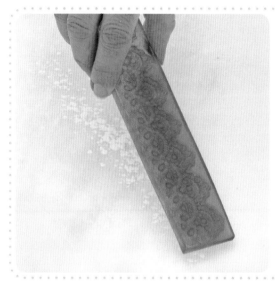

1 Dust the inside of the mold with cornstarch, and then tap on a hard surface to remove any excess. Roll out the Mexican paste as thin as you can on a hard surface dusted with cornstarch.

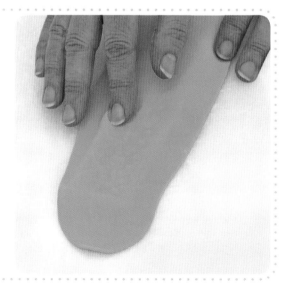

2 Carefully lift the rolled paste over the mold and use your fingers to press it into the grooves.

Variation

Use hard resin molds to create details, such as facial features and even heads. Resin allows your design to hold its shape better and minimizes distortion, making it ideal for lacework. Use vegetable shortening instead of cornstarch, if desired.

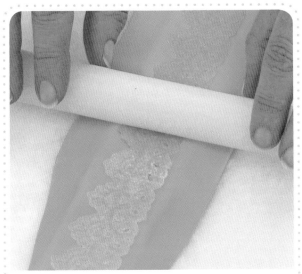

3 Lay the silicone insert on top of the paste and use the roller to push it downward, embossing the paste. Cut away the excess paste from the edges of the mold with a sharp knife.

4 Remove the silicone insert and rub the end of the ball tool over the raised areas to release any paste where there will be embossed details or cutaways.

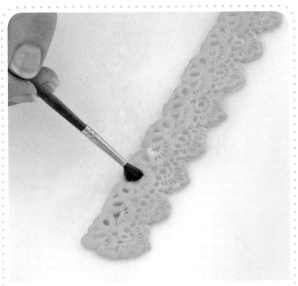

5 Run a wire brush over the whole surface of the paste to remove any loose pieces. Use a straight pin to lift up one end of the paste in the mold carefully, and then pull upward and out of the mold.

6 Brush with petal dust, if desired, and attach to the cake with edible glue or a little water, if preferred. Alternatively, you can dry the lace over a support for use with 3-D decorations.

STENCILING

Stenciling produces a magnificent series of textures, designs, and finishes on any frosted surface, with professional-looking and pristine results. You can use store-bought stencils in a myriad of ways—such as simple painted or dusted designs, royal-iced intricate damask-style patterns, and embossed features.

Stenciling the sides of a cake

Create beautiful designs on cakes or mini cakes using royal icing and a stencil. This is a technique that can take a little practice to get right, so do a few trial runs on a length of fondant before attempting to stencil directly onto your finished cake.

Equipment

* stencil
* masking tape
* fondant smoother

Ingredients

* confectioner's sugar, for dusting
* royal-iced or fondant-covered round cake
* royal icing, for piping (see p.35)
* coloring paste, optional

Tips

For a smoother finish and better ease of movement, use a flat-edged scraper or a stoneware scraper instead of a palette knife to apply the royal icing. If you smudge any of the icing, use a toothpick to scrape it away.

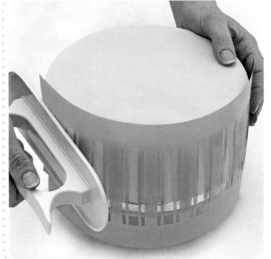

1 Dust the back of the stencil with a little confectioner's sugar. Place the stencil directly on the surface of the cake in the position you would like the design to appear. Use masking tape to secure the stencil into place on the cake. Use a fondant smoother to press down firmly on the stencil and emboss lightly.

2 Color your royal icing, if desired. Spread the royal icing thinly over the stencil, using the palette knife in one direction only. Let dry and then move the stencil, wipe it clean, and repeat as desired around the cake. Allow each design to set fully before moving the stencil, so that you do not smudge the pattern.

Stenciling with royal icing

This is a quick way to create detailed decorations for cakes. Make sure you use piping-consistency royal icing, or the icing may run under the edges of the stencil cutouts and smear the design. The icing should be roughly the consistency of toothpaste (see p.35).

Equipment

* stencil
* masking tape
* fondant roller

Ingredients

* confectioner's sugar
* fondant or royal-icing covered square cake
* royal icing, for piping (see p.35)

1 Dust the back of the stencil with a little confectioner's sugar to keep it from sticking to the surface of the cake. Place the stencil directly onto the surface of the cake, in the position you would like the design to appear. Use masking tape to hold the stencil in place.

A quick way to create detailed designs

2 Press the stencil down into the fondant and run the fondant roller over the top, so that the pattern is lightly embossed, with the fondant just rising above the surface of the stencil.

Tip
When the royal icing begins to form a crust on top of your stencil (step 3), you could apply petal dust to add color and texture. Rub a little vegetable shortening over the surface of the stencil. Use a large, soft brush to apply the dust.

3 Using a palette knife, spread the royal icing thinly over the surface of the stencil, using gentle strokes in one direction. Cover the whole stencil in icing to be sure you have not missed any parts of the design.

4 Leave the stencil in place for about 10 minutes, so that the icing begins to set. Carefully lift off the stencil, pulling upward from one corner and peeling it across, to reveal the design beneath.

Stenciling with paint

It is easier to stencil with paint than with royal icing, and you can achieve a variety of dramatic effects. Make sure the fondant or buttercream has set for at least 24 hours, so the surface has developed a crust beforehand. The food coloring paint needs to be thick to keep it from running.

Equipment
* stencil

Ingredients
* vegetable shortening, for greasing
* fondant-covered or smooth-frosted cake
* petal or luster dust mixed with grain alcohol, or vodka

...you can achieve a variety of dramatic effects

Variations
For quick and easy coverage, try airbrushing the stencil (see pp.144–45). Use thin coats and build up a final color. You could use undiluted airbrush paints with a paintbrush. Avoid water-based food-coloring paints or gels, since they can run.

1 Grease the back of the stencil with a little vegetable shortening and press it onto the cake in the desired position.

2 Dip a small paintbrush into a little paint. Paint around the edges of the pattern, onto the surface of the cake.

3 Next, paint inside the edges you have painted, using small, fine strokes to apply even coverage over the whole pattern.

4 Allow the paint to dry completely before removing the stencil. Fix mistakes with a cotton swab dipped in grain alcohol.

Stenciling with edible dust

You can use any dry edible dusts with a stencil, to create subtle patterns on the top and sides of your cake. Dust over the stencil or stipple with a wide brush, but make sure that you do not spill any onto the cake when lifting off the stencil.

Equipment
* stencil
* masking tape, optional

Ingredients
* vegetable shortening, for greasing
* fondant-covered or smooth-frosted cake
* pearl, luster, or petal dust

Create subtle patterns on the top and sides of a cake

Tip
If you are using a single stencil wrapped around the circumference of a fondant-covered cake, grease the back of the stencil with a little vegetable shortening so it will stick to the surface. Otherwise, use masking tape to secure it into place.

1 Grease the back of the stencil with a little vegetable shortening and press it onto the cake in the desired position. You could use a little masking tape to create "handles" on either side of the stencil. Place a little dust in a small strainer and gently shake it across the surface of the stencil.

2 Lift off the stencil, making sure that it remains flat so that none of the dust on the stencil drops onto the cake.

Stencil embossing

You can use an embossing technique with any stencil that will lie flat on the surface of a cake. Emboss the entire surface by embossing the fondant before using it to cover a cake, or emboss decorations, like this border, for a textured finish. Enhance your design with luster dust.

Equipment

* stencil
* fondant roller
* veining tool, optional

Ingredients

* vegetable shortening, for greasing
* length of rolled fondant, strengthened if desired (see p.87), or rolled buttercream (see p.27)
* petal dust

1 Lightly grease the surface of the fondant with a little vegetable shortening. This prevents the stencil from slipping and sticking to the surface of the fondant when it has been embossed, and also helps to fix any dusts you may wish to use after embossing.

Variations

Use edible felt-tip pens to paint the surface of embossed fondant, for subtle shading, or fully colored designs. Pens are easier to control than paintbrushes, particularly for intricate designs. Let each section dry before moving on to the next.

2 Place the stencil on the surface of the fondant and, using the roller, roll it firmly across the stencil, pressing it down so that fondant begins to poke out of the cutout edges. If you are using a large stencil on a length of rolled-out fondant, work from the inside of the stencil outward, until the entire surface is evenly embossed.

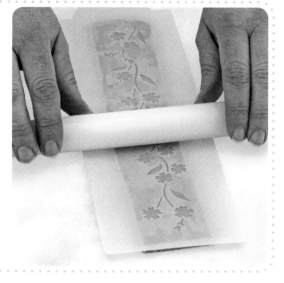

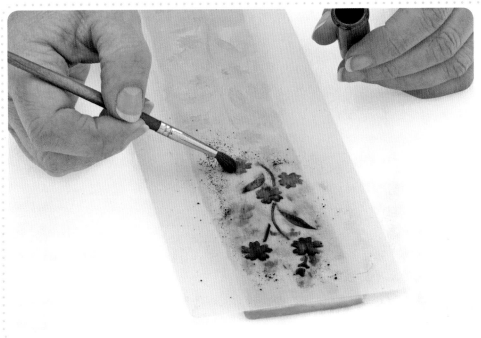

3 With a small paintbrush, dust the surface of the stencil with petal dust, using light strokes or stipples to ensure that the entire pattern is covered. Leave for 1–2 hours to allow the dust to set, and then use a soft brush to remove any excess.

4 Remove the stencil and use the end of a sharp knife, or a cotton swab, to clear away any areas where the dust has escaped the outlines of the design. If the pattern is unevenly embossed, or you wish to add more detail, use a veining tool to press down the fondant carefully around the design.

Stencil designs

Paint, dust, ice, airbrush, or spray stencils to create wonderful designs on cakes and decorations. You can also use them to emboss any medium, for a highly textured effect. Get the most from each stencil by repeating patterns or picking out particular details you like.

Butterfly
A diluted color wash gives this butterfly an ethereal look, which would work well on floral-themed cakes or cupcakes.

Damask
Paint or ice a line of these stencils around a wedding cake, or use, one by one, for the sides or tops of cakes and mini cakes, or as a fondant cupcake topper.

Crewel embroidery
Spread this stencil with white or tinted royal icing or carefully paint it with diluted dust. It would be beautiful on the sides or top of a cake.

Butterfly
Use luster spray to achieve an even coverage of the stenciled area. Repeat the pattern in different colors on cupcakes or around a cake.

Butterfly
Use a fine-tipped point brush to achieve delicate outlines for this pretty butterfly, and dot it among stenciled flowers and foliage.

Skull and crossbones

A color wash makes this image suitably weather-worn. Try on pirate cupcakes or the rice paper sails of a ship.

Imperial crown

Dilute luster dust with grain alcohol and stencil onto strengthened fondant, cut around, dry, and use as a cupcake topper.

Coronation crown

Brush with pale gold luster dust for a softer appearance or use to emboss the surface of cupcakes and mini cakes.

Violet wallpaper

Repeat this crewel embroidery pattern across the surface of a cake, brushing with lilac paint to create an elegant, antique wallpaper design.

Decorative roses

Sponge pink and green petal dusts, thinned with grain alcohol, to create a delicate spray of roses on a cake or cupcake top, or a simple plaque.

Russet sprigs

Select detail from a larger stencil and sponge or stipple with light and darker shades of the same color for a burnished appearance.

Tumbling teddy bears

Paint the teddy bears with soft aqua around the base of a fondant-covered cake or on a thin strip of gum paste. Individual bears make pretty toppers for cupcakes or mini cakes.

PAINTING

Achieve a spectacular finish and intricate, textured designs with painting or airbrushing. Paint your cakes and decorations with a range of edible dusts, tints, pastes, paints, and pens. Create smooth, flawless royal-icing run-outs, or dappled, dotted fondant surfaces. Use a variety of different textures and special effects to make your creations unique.

Using food coloring paints

Apply these ready-to-use edible paints to decorations with a brush or sponge (see p.147). Use a broad brush for easier application on large surfaces. It is best to cover as much of the decoration as you can with each stroke, since multiple layers can make the surface uneven.

Ingredients

* fondant ribbons
* food coloring paint
* grain alcohol or vodka

...cover as much of the decoration as you can with each stroke

1 Lay the ribbons on a flat surface, leaving a gap between each. Brush them with a soft brush to remove excess cornstarch. Shake the paint well before pouring a small amount onto a plate or paint palette. Dip a paintbrush in the paint and carefully apply to the sides of the ribbons using straight, even strokes.

Tips

Always clean the brushes with grain alcohol or vodka, since many paints harden in water, making the brush unusable. If the paint dries out while you are working, or it becomes too thick, stir in a little grain alcohol to thin it out.

2 Paint the top of the ribbons in the same way, ideally in just a few long strokes. If the finish is uneven, let the paint dry completely before adding a second coat. You can use these ribbons in so many ways—from bright stripes on a train cake, to wooden planks on a pirate ship cake.

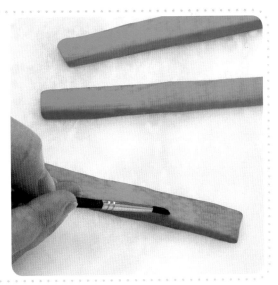

Using petal dusts

You can paint entire cakes with petal dusts, or simply add shimmer and color to small decorations. Paint made from petal dust dries very quickly, so use a little and work as fast as you can—it is better to use several coats of thin paint than to use one layer of thick paint.

Ingredients

* petal dust
* grain alcohol or vodka
* dry fondant or gum-paste decorations

...simply add shimmer and color

Variations

Mix dusts and powders to create new shades, or add luster dust for shimmer. To paint large areas with blended colors, mix up a large quantity, but add grain alcohol a little at a time. If the alcohol evaporates, add more to the powder if needed, or store away.

1 Place a small amount of dust in a ramekin and add a few drops of grain alcohol. Mix until smooth to create a "paint."

2 For overall color, apply the paint from the inside outward, to keep from forming a pool of paint in the center. Let dry.

3 Refresh the ramekin with alcohol. When the first coat is dry, paint another. Use a thin brush for detailing, if desired.

4 For a gentle tint or luster, allow the paint to dry and brush on dry dust rather than using the alcohol to create a paint.

Using edible pens

Use edible pens to paint fine details and write directly onto fondant or fondant-covered cakes and gum-paste decorations. Use the pens with stencils or on embossed surfaces to provide color and detail, or try them freehand. Most brands are available in broad or fine tips.

Ingredients

* dry fondant or gum-paste decorations
* edible pens
* grain alcohol or vodka, optional

...paint fine details and write directly onto fondant

Variations

Emboss a design onto a cake using a cutter or a template. Choose broad edible pens to color your work, using even strokes on small areas, and fine-tipped pens for crisp outlines. Dip a paintbrush in grain alcohol to smudge or thin the inked surfaces.

1 Place the decorations on a flat, firm surface and support any parts that might shift or wobble while you work. Fill in larger areas first, using a broad or fine pen, depending on the size of the area that needs coverage.

2 Use a finer pen to create outlines and finer details, highlight your work, provide contrast, or cover any messy edges. Store the pens upside down. If the pens form crystals, dip them in grain alcohol for a minute or two, put on the caps and shake. Let them rest for 15 minutes before using.

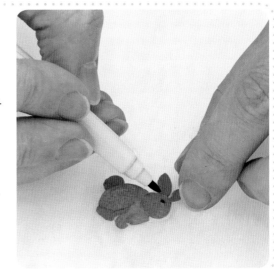

Using coloring pastes

Use coloring pastes for painting, as well as for adding color to frostings, modeling clays and pastes, and fondant. You can use more grain alcohol to create a thinner paint for color washes, stippling, or sponging, or less to create denser blocks of color with a paintbrush.

Ingredients

* coloring pastes
* grain alcohol or vodka
* fondant-covered cake, or fondant or gum-paste decoration

Vary shades to create contrasting effects

Tip

Coloring paste can be thinned with water, but it tends to give a less even coverage and have an increased drying time, so instead, mix with grain alcohol or vodka— great when you are under time pressure because it dries so much more quickly.

1 Use a toothpick to place a little coloring paste in a ramekin. Add a few drops of grain alcohol to the paste, then stir with the toothpick until absorbed and the paint is loose and smooth.

2 Apply the paint immediately with a paintbrush, adding a little more grain alcohol to keep it fluid.

Brushwork embroidery

Use royal icing to create beautiful, textured designs on a variety of cakes or decorations, with just a cutter and a paintbrush. This technique is called brushwork embroidery because the finished result is very much like a detailed, embroidered surface.

Equipment

* cutter, to emboss
* piping bag with narrow round piping tip

Ingredients

* fondant-covered or smooth-frosted cakes
* royal icing (colored, if desired; see pp.34–35), thinned with a little water

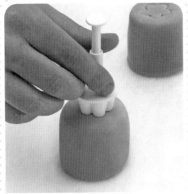

1 Lightly emboss an outline on the cake surface using a cutter. Allow the fondant to set for a few hours.

2 Fill the piping bag with royal icing. Working on one part of the design at a time, pipe over the embossed outline.

Tips

Keep the brush damp. You will be able to make 3 or 4 strokes before it needs to be dipped into water again. After the brushwork, pipe details, such as centers for flowers or stems for leaves, if desired. Let dry.

3 Dip a paintbrush in water and draw it through the icing toward the center of the design, using small, even strokes.

4 Continue to pull the icing into the center of the design, until the shape is complete. Pipe more detail onto the design.

Piping royal icing run-outs

Royal icing run-out, also known as "flood work," involves piping royal icing into a shape and allowing it to dry until hard. You can use the decoration as part of a 3-D cake topping, or lay it flat to embellish cakes, cookies, gingerbread, and cupcakes. Be careful, since it will be fragile.

Equipment

* food-grade acetate sheets
* cardboard or parchment paper template
* piping bags with small, fine, circular piping tip and large circular piping tip

Ingredients

* vegetable shortening, for greasing
* royal icing (see pp.34–35), tinted or colored, as desired

1 Lay the acetate sheet directly onto the template so that the template is visible through the surface. Lightly grease the acetate with vegetable shortening. You can also lay the template on top of a piece of parchment paper and trace the shape, if preferred.

2 Using the small, fine tip, pipe royal icing around the outline of the shape. Allow this to dry for a couple of hours to create a "dam," or if you are using different colors on the surface of your decoration, pipe in outlines now, and then let everything dry.

Variations

For thick, sturdy run-outs, apply several coats of piped icing. Allow each coat to dry for 24 hours. Produce multicolored run-outs by filling areas with royal icing in different colors. As long as there is no break in the outline, the icing will hold its shape.

3 The royal icing needs to be thinned for the run-out stage. Spritz the royal icing with water, or add it drop by drop until the icing is roughly the consistency of shampoo. Draw a spoon through the surface. If the line created fills in 10 seconds, it is the right consistency for flooding. Fill a piping bag attached to the large tip, with the thin royal icing. Press down on the piping bag and "flood" the template with icing, working from the center outward until the entire surface of the design is covered. When the flooding is complete, gently tap the board or surface beneath the shape to release any air bubbles that will make the shape more fragile.

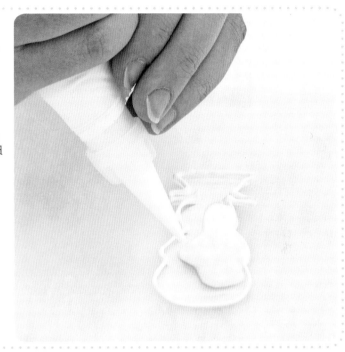

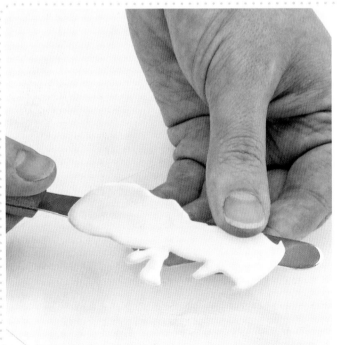

4 Allow to dry for 24 hours before applying details, such as additional piping or painting. Lift the decoration away from the acetate sheet with a palette knife and carefully apply to the cake with a dab of royal icing. Alternatively, you could attach to a cake-pop stick or wire with a dab of royal icing.

Run-out designs *are easily layered (see pp.220–22).*

Painting flowers

Tinting or painting flowers makes them look realistic, even if you have used colored fondant or modeling paste. You can dust flowers and leaves molded from gum paste in the same way—and you can go one step further by steaming them lightly to add sheen.

Equipment

* Styrofoam or floral foam, optional

Ingredients

* gum-paste roses, or fondant or other modeling-paste flowers; wired, if desired
* petal dust or pearl dust
* grain alcohol or vodka, optional

Steam flowers lightly to add sheen

Tips

Do not steam the flower for longer than a few seconds or it may disintegrate. As soon as it takes on a light sheen, remove it from the steam and place it on parchment paper or floral foam to dry. Hold the wire with tongs.

1 Lay the flowers on a flat surface. They will need to be completely dry. If the flowers are wired, place them in floral foam so that they stand upright.

2 Place some petal dust on a plate and dip a paintbrush into it. Apply carefully to the inside of the petals, and work outward, pulling the brush along the surface of the petals to the edge. Use slightly darker tints of the same color at the center of the petals and along the top edges to provide realistic contrast and definition.

3 Apply the dust to the outside of the flower in small, even strokes, working from the bottom to the top. If desired, mix together a little dust with some grain alcohol (see p.136) to create a smooth paint, and apply this where you want the colors to be darkest—at the base of the petals, for example. If your flowers are made from fondant or modeling paste, don't steam them (see below). Instead, allow to dry overnight before applying to your cake.

To steam gum-paste flowers, fill a small pan with water and bring to a boil. Hold each flower over the steam for a few seconds, until the paste takes on a wet appearance. This sets the dust and the color. Turn the flower to make sure all surfaces come into contact with the steam.

Gum-paste orchids *can also be tinted (see pp.90–91).*

Airbrushing

Use an airbrushing machine to create an even base color for frosted cakes, or to add detail and shading to cakes, stencil designs, and decorations. Although airbrushing can take time to master (practice on paper towel or newspaper), the results are well worth the effort.

Equipment

* airbrushing machine

Ingredients

* fondant-covered cake
* food coloring paints
* grain alcohol
  or vodka, optional

...create an even base color for frosted cakes

Variation

Use airbrushing to give definition to 3-D cakes and decorations; for example, spray a darker orange into the grooves of a pumpkin, add a lighter shade to the center surface of a balloon, use for a detailed stencil, or give detail to a handbag cake.

1 Cover the area around the cake, including the board, with newspaper or parchment paper. Load the airbrushing machine with the food coloring paint. Holding the nozzle about 8in (20cm) from the cake and at a 45° angle, spray all over the top using long, sweeping movements.

2 Allow the layer to dry. Remove the paint and clean out the pipes of the machine to ensure that the colors do not run and the needle is clean enough to provide a uniform, even spray. Load the next color into the machine.

3 Holding the nozzle at a 90° angle will create a more defined line, which is perfect for this rainbow design. Starting at the bottom, spray the first color, changing the angle of the nozzle to produce the desired effect.

4 Clean the machine again and load the next color, spraying this next to the first color as evenly as possible. It is better to layer light swathes of color than to spray too much at once.

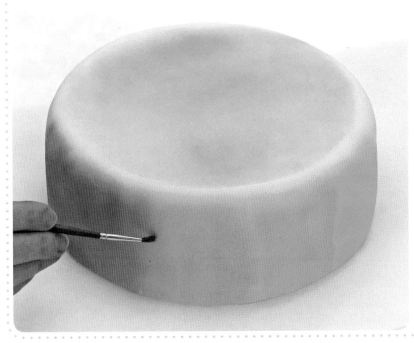

5 Continue until all the colors are in place. You could neaten the edges of the design with the blade of a sharp knife or blur the edges a little with a paintbrush dipped in grain alcohol (as shown here).

Tips

You can make colors darker by retracing over them with the airbrushing machine. Unless you wish to create a secondary color, try to keep from spraying one color on top of another, since they will blend and create new color shades.

Painting a color wash

Color washes can highlight embossing, pick out textures on decorations, and provide a light background for further design work. You will need very diluted ready-made paint, or you can mix your own from coloring dust or paste and grain alcohol (see p.136 and p.138).

Ingredients

* ❋ food coloring paint, coloring paste, or dusts in 2 colors
* ❋ grain alcohol or vodka
* ❋ embossed fondant-covered cake

...provide a light background for further design work

Variations

"Drag" by painting the surface with 1 color, and gently brushing the cake in one direction and then the other, using a clean, dry paintbrush. "Rag-roll" by using a balled-up piece of paper towel to apply and remove paint and create a mottled effect.

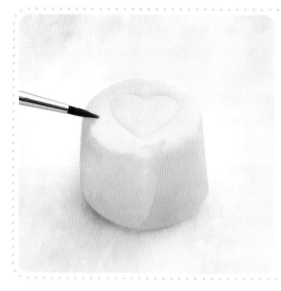

1 Dilute the paint with grain alcohol to prepare a wash. Using a paintbrush, wash the paint over the surface of the embossed cake. Cover evenly or unevenly, depending on the look you want. For a dark shade, color-wash the cake a second time and allow the excess paint to pool in the embossed grooves.

2 Paint some of the smaller areas or detailed sections of your embossed design, such as this heart, with another color wash. You may want to use a smaller brush for finer details like this. Let dry.

Stippling and sponging

These methods help you to create different textures on the surface of cakes or decorations. Use a stippling brush or specialized sponge to produce a subtle finish with tiny dots of color. Sponging achieves a dappled result; try playing around with layers in different shades.

Equipment

* stippling brush or sponge
* sponge

Ingredients

* edible liquid paint, coloring paste, or dusts
* grain alcohol or vodka
* fondant-covered or smooth-frosted cake or rolled fondant

...create different textures on the surface of cakes

Tips

Stipple, wash, or sponge shades of the same color in layers to produce a textured look. Try sponging a lighter shade of a color over a darker base to create the look of fabric. Dab the sponge heavily over some parts to make a velvet effect.

1 **To stipple**, lightly dip the stippling brush into food coloring paint that is heavily diluted with grain alcohol.

2 Dot your brush on the surface of the cake in an up-and-down motion. Let dry and repeat, if desired.

1 **To sponge**, you can use thicker paint for a bolder result. Dip the sponge into the paint and apply to the cake.

2 Rinse your sponge. Apply a second color for a textured look. To prevent muddying, let dry before applying new colors.

IMAGING

*Digital imaging—on edible frosting or rice paper—
has transformed the cake-decorating world. Make
your creations personal and add accurate details
using images or patterns. Print at home on an adapted
printer or commission a specialty supplier to create
images that can be attached to your cakes.*

Using rice paper

Rice paper is available in different colors, patterns, and pretty prints. It can be folded and bent without cracking, which makes it perfect for these butterfly designs. Decorate with edible glitter, if you like, and attach them to cakes with royal icing or edible glue.

Ingredients

* sheet of rice paper, printed with edible ink
* piping gel
* edible glitter

You can fold or bend rice paper designs without cracking them

1 Lay out your rice paper sheet on a flat surface and cut out the images carefully. Transfer them onto parchment paper until you want to use them for decorating. For a sparkly touch, prepare the shapes by painting them with piping gel and letting them dry for a few hours, ideally overnight.

2 When the gel is gummy, sprinkle edible glitter over the top. You can fold the paper gently, if appropriate, for a 3-D effect—perfect here for the butterfly wings. Let the butterflies dry in the crease of an open hardback book so they dry in shape, then attach to your cake with royal icing or edible glue.

Variation

If you are printing on rice paper yourself—using a printer set up with edible ink—make sure the rice paper is sturdy enough to absorb the ink without dissolving. Check with the supplier to ensure that the paper is appropriate for printing.

Using edible images

Send your images to a company specializing in edible ink products to have your edible image printed. Cut them out and apply directly to your cake top—or stick them to sturdy gum paste or strengthened fondant first. The sheets must be kept in a zippered bag or they will dry out.

Equipment

* fondant roller

Ingredients

* printed edible images
* cornstarch, for dusting
* strengthened fondant (see p.87)
* cupcakes piped with buttercream frosting, optional

...apply images to rolled, strengthened fondant

Tips

You can wrap edible images with ready-printed patterns on them around the sides of your cake. Why not try leopard print for a handbag cake, or fairies and butterflies for a little girl's cake? The possiblities are endless.

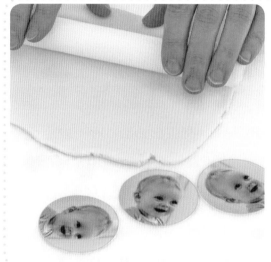

1 Carefully cut out all the images from the edible sheet with scissors and set aside. Dust a surface with cornstarch and roll out the fondant to the desired thickness.

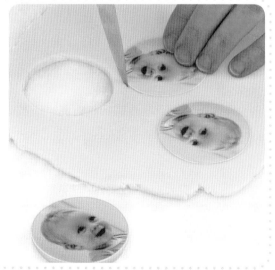

2 Moisten the surface of the fondant with a little water, using a pastry brush, and then arrange the images on top, as closely together as possible. Allow to dry for a few minutes and then cut out the mages on the fondant, using a sharp knife.

3 Place the images on a piece of parchment paper, image side up, and allow to dry overnight, until hard.

4 Affix the images to the frosted cupcakes, if desired, by moistening the back of the fondant with water using a pastry brush, and pressing into place.

Variation

You can print edible images yourself with lettering and/or images, but to do that you would need a specially adapted printer with edible ink. Alternatively, email your design to a specialty company that will print it for you.

FINISHING TOUCHES

That finishing touch makes all the difference to your cake. From spray-glazing to spinning sugar, the techniques are simple and the results are showstopping. Insert ribbons and fresh flowers, decorate with silver dragées and edible diamonds or gems, and transform your cake or decoration into a work of art.

Working with edible glitter

You can dust cakes with edible glitter dust and make sugar decorations even prettier with edible glitter flakes. You can also add glitter to piping gel or royal icing, to highlight embossed shapes, such as this heart, or to use for piping shimmering lettering.

Equipment

* cutter, to emboss
* piping bag with round piping tip

Ingredients

* piping gel or royal icing
* edible glitter flakes
* edible glitter dust
* fondant or gum-paste plaque, or other decoration

...make sugar decorations prettier with glitter flakes

Variation

Use a small paintbrush to apply edible glue to the surface of a decoration, or onto embossed lines on a decoration or cake, and cover well with a few shakes of glitter flakes or dust. Let dry and, using a large, soft brush, gently remove any excess.

1 Use a paintbrush to mix piping gel with the flakes and/or dust, until you achieve your desired look. Piping gel does not set hard, so for a firmer result use royal icing instead. Emboss a fondant plaque or decoration with a cookie cutter.

2 Fill a piping bag with the glitter mixture, as prepared above. Pipe into the lines embossed on the plaque or decoration and let set overnight.

Using edible gems

Adorn your cupcakes with realistic edible jewels. Keep edible gems, such as these edible diamonds, in an airtight container and place them on the cupcake or decoration at the very last minute, or they will cloud. Use tweezers, rather than your fingers, to apply.

Equipment
* fondant roller
* large plunger cutter
* tweezers

Ingredients
* cornstarch, for dusting
* strengthened fondant (see p.87)
* cupcakes piped with buttercream frosting
* royal icing (see pp.34–35)
* large edible diamonds

...place realistic edible jewels on your cupcakes at the last minute

1 Dust a surface with cornstarch and roll out the fondant to the desired thickness. Use a plunger cutter to cut out shapes, such as these daisies. Let dry, until just beginning to harden.

2 Moisten the back of each shape with water and apply to the top of your cupcakes. Place a small amount of royal icing in the center of each daisy. Top with an edible diamond.

Inserting ribbons

This technique works best on a cake that has been covered completely with fondant and left to rest for at least one day. Make sure you have enough ribbon to wrap all the way around the cake. You could easily insert ribbons onto the top of your cake, too.

Equipment

* knife with flat-ended blade
* tweezers
* ribbon, cut into ½in (1cm) lengths

Ingredients

* fondant-covered cake

Variations

For edible alternatives, you can create ribbons with gum paste (see pp.118–19) and insert them carefully while they are still soft and pliable. You could also cut printed edible images (see pp.150–51) into ribbons and insert those.

1 Use the knife to make small cuts in the fondant covering, about 1in (2.5cm) from the bottom. Cut the slots in pairs, about ¼in (5mm) wide and ½in (1cm) apart. Make sure the length of each slot is slightly longer than the width of the ribbon.

2 Use the tweezers to insert one end of a ribbon piece carefully into the top slot. Curve the ribbon downward and feed the other end into the lower slot. Repeat around the bottom of the cake until all the slots are filled with ribbon. Gently smooth down the pieces of ribbon with your fingers.

Quilting and adding dragées

Quilting produces an embossed pattern and is great for novelty designs, such as handbag cakes. Use a stitching tool and a printed mat to help you achieve a neat, regular pattern. You can press dragées (hard sugar balls with a metallic sugar coating) into the quilted corners.

Equipment

* fondant mat, marked with squares or diamonds
* fondant roller
* stitching (quilting) tool
* scraper or ruler to use for a straight edge
* 2in (5cm) circle cutter
* tweezers

Ingredients

* cornstarch, for dusting
* fondant
* fondant-covered cake, decorated with ribbon, if desired
* silver dragées

Tip

You can use royal icing to attach dragées more securely. Work quickly—it hardens fast, making it difficult for the dragées to stick. If you find this tricky, try adding a dot of piping gel to the royal icing—this will keep it moist for longer.

1 Dust the mat with cornstarch and roll out the fondant. Score a series of lines using the stitching tool and the edge of a scraper.

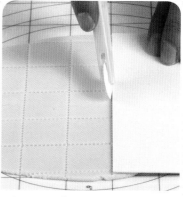

2 Using the scraper, score a series of vertical lines into the fondant. Ensure that the gap between each line is the same.

3 Cut out a circle of fondant, using the cutter. Lift it over the cake with a palette knife. Smooth down carefully.

4 Press dragées onto the quilted circle using tweezers. Cover a whole crumb-coated cake with the quilted fondant, if preferred.

Crimping

Crimpers are small tools, like tongs, with patterned edges. They are used to imprint patterns on fondant-covered cake drums, cakes, or decorations. The rubber bands on the arms determine the width of the pattern imprinted on the cake. Use crimpers while the fondant is still soft.

Equipment

* crimper
* natural bristle pastry brush

Ingredients

* fondant-covered cake drum, or cake
* luster dust

...imprint patterns on fondant-covered cake drums and cakes

Tips

All luster dusts can be mixed with grain alcohol or vodka to make an edible paint (see p.136). Mix pearl and petal or blossom dusts to create a tinted, gentle shine. Knead dusts into fondant or molten white chocolate for a hint of sparkle.

1 Position the crimper at a 90° angle above the surface of the cake drum. Press halfway into the fondant, but not all the way through to the drum. Squeeze gently, and then release the arms.

2 Carefully remove the crimper from the fondant and repeat the technique until you have the desired look. Be careful not to remove the crimper before you release the pressure, or you will damage the fondant. Using the pastry brush, apply the luster dust.

Spinning sugar

Spun sugar can produce a variety of different decorative touches. Use it to create smoke for a chimney, a nest for sugar birds or eggs, or a spider's web. Brushing the pan with cold water prevents the sugar from crystallizing. Spun sugar hardens in minutes, so work quickly.

Equipment

* natural bristle pastry brush
* candy thermometer

Ingredients

* 1¼ cups granulated sugar
* 1 cup water

*...create smoke,
delicate nests,
or a spider's web*

Variation

To make spun-sugar trees, add a few drops of green coloring paste to the sugar and water before you heat them. Follow the method up to step 3, then gently press the sugar strands into a cone shape around a cake-pop stick. Allow to harden.

1 Gently heat the sugar and water in a heavy-bottomed pan. Do not stir. Dip a brush in cold water and brush the sides of the pan.

2 Continue to cook the mixture until it reaches 311°F (155°C). Take the pan off the heat and plunge into a bowl of water.

3 Dip a fork into the syrup, then quickly whip the syrup back and forth over a rolling pin to create strands.

4 Gather the strands with your hands and shape as desired. Place on parchment paper to cool and harden completely.

Spraying with mists and glazes

Finish cakes with a beautiful, food color mist spray. You can use a variety of solid colors to spray the surface of your cakes—these also come in metallic or pearlescent finishes. A clear glaze spray can also be used to provide sheen and highlights.

Equipment

* tweezers, optional

Ingredients

* fondant-covered cake
* food color mist spray
* glaze spray
* royal icing (see pp.34–35)
* silver dragées, optional

Use a luster spray for a metallic or pearlescent coating

Tip

You can use glaze spray, also known as confectioner's spray, to add shine to chocolate that may get marked with fingerprints. Glaze sprays are preferable to brushed glazes because they offer an even finish that only takes moments to dry.

1 Place the cakes on a sheet of parchment paper to protect the work surface and allow you to move them easily after spraying.

2 Shake the spray can and hold it about 6in (15cm) away from the cake. Lightly mist over the surface for a subtle tint.

3 Allow to dry and then spray with glaze for a uniform, shiny appearance. Decorate as soon as the glaze is dry.

To add dragées, dot royal icing around the base of each cake at regular intervals. Using tweezers, press a dragée into each dot.

Displaying sugar flowers

You can adorn cakes with sugar flowers using a little royal icing. If you want to attach flower sprays, however, you will need to use flower picks as a safety measure. Group the sprays, sticking them into floral foam, to practice the bouquet you want before affixing it to the cake.

Equipment

* cake drum
* turntable or lazy Susan
* wire cutters
* food-safe flower picks

Ingredients

* frosted cake
* gum-paste or fondant flowers and foliage, on wires (see pp.88–89)
* edible glue, optional
* clear glaze spray, optional

Variation

To create a bouquet, start with leaves at the bottom. Put the large flowers in the center, then add the rest of the flowers and foliage. Wrap the stems with a length of fondant ribbon and a bow. Lightly brush the top of the cake with water and lay the bouquet on top.

1 Place the cake and its drum on the turntable. Put the largest flower in a flower pick and insert it into the top of the cake edge.

2 Select some smaller flowers and place them in a flower pick. Arrange them on the cake so that all the wires are covered.

3 Continue to add flowers, filling the gaps. Add the foliage, putting the wires into flower picks and repeating the process.

4 If desired, spray the flower display lightly with clear glaze spray (see p.159) to seal and add shine.

Displaying fresh flowers

Fresh flowers have a striking impact and can give a sense of the season to cakes. Edible flowers, such as roses, pansies, and lilac, are the perfect choice. Never push flower stems directly into the cake; use flower picks instead.

Equipment

* ❋ secateurs or scissors
* ❋ turntable or lazy Susan
* ❋ food-safe flower picks
* ❋ piping bag and tip, optional

Ingredients

* ❋ fresh flowers (edible, if desired) soaked in tepid water for 1 hour
* ❋ frosted or fondant-covered cake
* ❋ chocolate or other flavoured buttercream frosting (see pp.24–25)

Variation

You can use floral foam soaked in water and a plastic plate to create a display on your cake. Affix the plate to the top of the cake with buttercream and place the foam on top. Push a dowel through the foam, plate, and cake. Press flower stems into the foam.

1 Pat the flowers dry and cut stems to the desired length. Place the cake on the turntable so that you can access all sides easily. Fill the flower picks with a little water and press the stem of a flower into each one.

2 One-by-one, press the picks into the sides of the cake at a downward angle so the picks cannot be seen. Continue around the cake until you have a uniform ring of flowers. Pipe a little chocolate buttercream over any places where the picks are evident. Mist with a light spray of water.

PROJECTS

Create a stunning array of celebration cakes for virtually any occasion. Step-by-step instructions and helpful tips ensure success. Whether you want to decorate a cake for a wedding, child's birthday party, or Christmas celebration, you'll find everything you need to make the cake of your dreams—as well as many ideas for other delightful cakes.

Train cake

This cute train is covered in smooth blue fondant, with painted, gum-paste and fondant features glued into place with a little water. Let loose on his edible track, he'll be sure to please a crowd of little ones.

TIMING allow 1½ days, including drying time

SERVES 25

Equipment

* fondant roller
* 14in (35cm) round cake drum
* woodwork texture sheet
* multi-ribbon cutter
* circle cutters: 2¼in (6cm), 2¾in (7cm), 1¾in (4.5cm), and 1½in (4cm)
* veining tool
* round piping tip (such as PME no. 1)
* 3ft (1m) green satin ribbon (½in/1cm wide)
* craft glue

1 Two days before serving, roll out the lime green fondant on a cornstarch-dusted surface and cover the drum (see p.51), leaving a 4in (10cm) gap for the tracks. Strengthen 3½oz (100g) of the black fondant, roll it out, and cut a strip to fill the gap. Roll out the gray fondant, then cut 2 strips, 1in (2.5cm) wide. Place on the black fondant as rails. Roll out the brown fondant and emboss with the texture sheet. Cut 10 strips, ¾in x 4in (2cm x 10cm) in size. Moisten and place across the track, as slats. Set aside to dry.

2 Strengthen 7oz (200g) of the yellow fondant (see p.87) and roll it out to ⅙in (4mm) thick. Use the cutters to cut four 2¼in (6cm) circles and two 2¾in (7cm) circles. Cut the sheet of gum paste into fine strips with the ribbon cutter and attach to the circles as spokes. Cut 6 more strips, wider than the depth of the circles, and fix them around the wheels. Let dry overnight.

3 Halve the cake, to make two 5in (12.5cm) slabs. Halve one of those slabs, to make two 2½in (6.5cm) pieces. Sandwich the smaller pieces together with buttercream and attach on top of the large slab to create the cabin. Freeze until just firm, and then carve the top of the tall end into a gentle curve. Crumb-coat the whole cake with buttercream (see p.29), and let set for 30 minutes.

BRING IT ALL TOGETHER

Using multi-ribbon cutters *see p.118*

Using cookie cutters *see pp.106–07*

Carving and covering cakes *see p.65*

Ingredients

- cornstarch, for dusting
- 14oz (400g) lime green fondant, strengthened
- tylose powder
- 7oz (200g) black fondant
- 3½oz (100g) gray fondant, strengthened
- 5½oz (150g) brown fondant, strengthened
- 14oz (400g) yellow fondant
- 2½oz (75g) sheet of black gum paste
- 10in (25cm) pound cake, 3in (7.5cm) deep
- 1½ cups buttercream
- 1lb 5oz (600g) blue fondant
- 14oz (400g) red fondant
- black petal dust
- superwhite icing whitener
- grain alcohol or vodka
- 2½oz (75g) white fondant

Tip

To make the cowcatcher at the front, strengthen the white fondant and form into a block. Use a knife to cut a shape that is triangular in front, with a flat top and sides. Moisten it with water, then cover the white shape with yellow fondant.

4 On a cornstarch-dusted surface, roll out the blue fondant to ⅙in (4mm) thick. Cover the cake and transfer it to the cake drum. Decorate the front of the train with 2 black fondant strips (⅝in x 2¼in/1.5cm x 6cm). Strengthen the remaining blue fondant and roll out a thick cylinder, 2¾in (7cm) wide. Moisten the base and attach to the train. Decorate it with 4 evenly spaced strips (½in/1cm wide) and a 1¾in (4.5cm) circle of red fondant. Cut another strip of red fondant (1½in/4cm wide) to fix around the base of the train. Attach this, then fix the wheels on top.

5 Strengthen and roll out the remaining red fondant to ⅙in (4mm) thick. Cut a rectangle about ⅙in (4mm) wider than the curved top of the train's cabin. Allow it to firm up for 20 minutes, and then fix it to the cake to form the cabin roof. Roll together the excess red fondant and model into a cone shape for the chimney, about 1½in (4cm) wide at the base and 2in (5cm) tall. Cut off each end to get a flat top and bottom. Decorate with a strip of blue fondant and a circle of yellow fondant. Set aside.

6 Cut a 1½in (4cm) circle from yellow fondant, score a smile with a veining tool, and fix to the front. Use a piping tip to cut 8 small circles from the yellow fondant, and fix these to the center of the wheels, and to the front of the cabin. Mark the windows on each side of the cabin and a curved window on the front with a sharp knife. Mix black petal dust and a little superwhite icing whitener together with grain alcohol, and paint the windows. Allow each to dry, then edge with thin strips of black fondant.

7 Cut a base for the chimney out of black fondant and fix to its base, then stick the entire chimney to the train. Emboss the top with the 1¾in (4.5cm) cutter. Affix a tiny circle of black fondant above the smile and create the eyes (see Tip, p.166).

8 Model the cowcatcher (see Tip, left) and attach it to the front of the train. To decorate it, roll out some red fondant and cut 11 thin strips. Apply one to the center of the cowcatcher, then fix on the rest at even intervals. Trim with black fondant.

9 Strengthen the remaining blue fondant and roll out to ¹⁄₁₆in (2mm) thick. Cut 2 strips, ½in (1cm) wide, and 7in (17cm) long. Let them dry for 20 minutes, and then attach them across both sets of wheels. Glue the ribbon around the cake drum.

Train cake pp.164–65

Tip

To create the eyes for the train, cut two eye shapes from rolled fondant and attach to the window. Mix together a little black dust with grain alcohol and paint the pupils. Dab flecks of superwhite and grain alcohol to create the gleam.

Dinosaur cake pp.168–69

Dinosaur cake

Crouched on a marbled board dotted with fondant rocks, this fierce little dinosaur will delight younger children. The cake is made using two bowl-shaped cakes (see Tip), then carved and covered with tinted fondant.

🕐 **TIMING** allow 1½ days, including drying time

 **SERVES** 30

Equipment

* fondant roller
* 14in (35cm) cake drum
* veining tool
* ball tool
* 3ft (1m) stone-colored satin ribbon (½in/1cm wide)
* craft glue

Ingredients

* 1lb 5oz (600g) white fondant (reserve 1oz/25g)
* tylose powder
* 7oz (200g) chocolate brown fondant
* cornstarch, for dusting

1 A day before you want to serve the cake, strengthen the white fondant with a little tylose powder, kneading it in well (see p.87). Marble it with the chocolate brown fondant (see p.47), carefully roll it out on a cornstarch-dusted surface, and cover the cake drum (see p.51). Set aside to harden for a day.

2 Place the smaller bowl cake in the freezer and, when firm, carve into the head shape. Crumb-coat it in buttercream frosting (see p.29). Apply strips of gooseberry-green fondant around the eyes and nose, to build up these areas. Set aside for about 30 minutes, or until the buttercream frosting has just set.

3 Place the large cake upside down and crumb-coat with buttercream frosting. Strengthen a length of gooseberry-green fondant (see p.87) and form into a cone shape for the tail.

4 Roll out the remaining gooseberry-green fondant on a cornstarch-dusted surface to ⅙in (4mm) thick, and cover the head and body, working from the top to the bottom. Smooth downward as you go. Cut off any excess and press the edges under the base of the body with the back of a knife. Join the tail to the body and smooth the seam with your fingers. Transfer the

BRING IT ALL TOGETHER

Covering a cake drum *see p.51*

Carving and covering cakes *see p.65*

Dusting with petal dust *see p.136*

* 2½ cup bowl cake, in vanilla sponge cake (see p.228)
* 1 cup buttercream frosting, to crumb-coat (see p.29)
* 3lb 3oz (1.5kg) gooseberry-green fondant
* 3½ cup bowl cake, in vanilla sponge (see p.228)
* ½oz (12g) pale blue fondant
* ½oz (12g) black fondant
* confectioner's glaze
* 2½oz (75g) pale gooseberry-green fondant
* moss-green petal dust
* 7oz (200g) gray fondant

dinosaur to the covered cake drum. Use the veining tool to tuck under the edges and your fingers to smooth the fondant where it meets the cake drum.

5 Use the veining tool to mark an incision that will become the mouth. Use the ball tool to create nostrils and to create ellipse-shaped sockets for the eyes.

6 Strengthen the remaining gooseberry-green fondant and form 4 legs, using about 7oz (200g) of fondant per leg. Make a tapered sausage for each leg. Flatten the narrower end for the foot and use a sharp knife to cut 3 toes into the end of each. Press each foot upward and score the ankles and the upper thighs with the veining tool, to give a wrinkled effect. Moisten the thigh-end of the legs with some water and attach them to the base of the body, curving the legs slightly outward.

7 Strengthen the reserved white fondant (see p.87) and use your hands to model 2 rounded ellipses with pointed sides, to fit into the eye sockets. Moisten the back of the eyes with some water and press into the sockets, allowing them to bulge out. Cut 2 irises from the pale blue fondant and press into place. Cut 2 strips of black fondant, moisten the backs, and fix to the eyes for the pupils. Brush with 2 coats of confectioner's glaze.

8 Strengthen the pale gooseberry-green fondant (see p.87), then form into 11 cones in descending sizes, using your fingers. Flatten and then cut off the widest end to create a flat edge on each. Roll one into a horn for the nose and curve it slightly backward. Allow to dry for 20 minutes, and then moisten the base of each and fix onto the head and spine of the dinosaur.

9 Using a larger brush, dust the body with moss-green edible petal dust, guiding the brush into all the crevices, to add depth and texture. Use the veining tool to create more ridges, if required.

10 Knead the gray fondant and, using your hands, form into different-shaped rocks. Dot around the covered cake drum.

11 Cut a length of ribbon to fit around the circumference of the cake drum, then affix it into place with craft glue, making sure that the seam is at the back.

Tip

Baking a cake in an ovenproof dish involves the same steps as baking half of a ball cake (see p.237). You need to insert a heat conductor, such as a slim skewer, into the center of the batter before it is baked, to ensure that it bakes evenly.

Princess castle

This castle cake is the ideal centerpiece for a fairy-tale party. The base cake is layered with fondant shapes to create an idyllic backdrop, and an exquisite hand-carved and modeled castle sits on top. Finish it with a little princess (see pp.92–93), complete with crown.

TIMING allow 4 days, including drying time

SERVES 25

Equipment

* fondant roller
* 14in (35cm) round cake drum
* frilling tool
* piping bag with fine tip (such as PME no. 1)
* sheet of cardboard
* masking tape
* cutting wheel
* 2 fondant smoothers
* 9in (23cm) round cake board

1 Four days before you wish to serve the cake, dust a flat surface with cornstarch, roll out the leaf-green fondant, and use to cover the cake drum (see p.51). Set aside to dry for 4 days.

For the princess

2 Model the basic figure on pp.92–93. Cut out a small heart from pink fondant and stick it to the center of the bodice. Use the frilling tool to form curls at the base of the strands of hair. Make the crown by rolling a piece of fondant that is wide enough to sit on the front of the head. Let dry and paint with gold luster dust mixed with grain alcohol. Pipe dots of frosting onto the tip of the crown, and fix to the hair with edible glue.

For the castle

3 Create a forming cone for the large turret (see Tip, opposite). Grease the outside of the cone lightly with vegetable shortening.

METHOD CONTINUES · · · ·

BRING IT ALL TOGETHER

Modeling a basic figure *see p.92-93*

Creating strong 3-D objects *see p.64*

Making a template *see p.57*

Stacking cakes with dowels *see p.68*

Tip

To make a forming cone, cut out a 9in (23cm) circle from cardboard. Make a single cut from one edge of the circle to the center. Form a cone approximately 5in (12.5cm) in diameter at the base. Secure with masking tape and trim the base.

* 5in (12.5cm) round
  cake board
* circle cutters, 1¾in
  (4.5cm), ¼in (5mm), and
  ½in (1cm) in diameter
* 8 dowels
* template for base cake
  design (see pp.244–45)
* blossom plunger
  cutter, small
* heart-shaped plunger
  cutters, small, medium,
  large, and extra large
* multi-ribbon cutter,
  straight and wavy edges
* 3ft (1m) pink satin
  ribbon (½in/1cm wide)
* craft glue

Ingredients

* cornstarch, for dusting
* 2lb 2oz (1kg) leaf-green
  fondant
* gold luster dust
* grain alcohol or vodka
* royal icing, for piping
  (see p.35)
* edible glue
* vegetable shortening,
  for greasing
* confectioner's sugar,
  for dusting
* 1lb 2oz (500g) Mexican
  paste (see p.53), in pink
* 3lb 3oz (1.5kg) pale
  blue fondant
* 9in (23cm) two-layer,

4 Dust a flat surface with confectioner's sugar, and roll out the pink Mexican paste. Using a cutting wheel, cut a 9in (23cm) circle and, as you did with the cardboard, cut a single straight line from the edge to the center of the circle. Working quickly, lift the paste carefully onto the cardboard cone and draw one edge over the other. Trim off any excess paste, allowing a ¼in (6mm) overlap. Affix in place with edible glue. Let dry for at least 3 days.

5 Roll out the pale blue fondant to ⅙in (4mm) thick on a cornstarch-dusted surface and cover the 9in (23cm) cake, using the fondant smoother to achieve a smooth surface (see p.50). Place the cake on its board and let dry overnight.

6 Using a very wide palette knife, transfer the frosted cake to the covered cake drum, placing it toward the back to leave space in the front for the princess and mini cupcakes, if desired.

7 Roll out the ivory fondant. Place the 5in (12.5cm) cake on its board and use the fondant to cover the cake, using 2 fondant smoothers to get a sharp, crisp top edge (see p.50).

8 Use a 1¾in (4.5cm) circle cutter to cut 20 circles from the slab of pound cake. Sandwich each with buttercream frosting, and create 4 towers, each a little over 5in (12.5cm) in height. Set them next to the small ivory cake to measure them—they should be exactly the same height as the fondant-covered cake on its board. Trim if necessary.

9 Insert a dowel into the center of each tower, laying them on their sides so that the dowel pokes out from the top and bottom. Crumb-coat the towers with buttercream frosting (see p.29). Roll out the remaining ivory fondant and cover the towers by wrapping strips around the outside, and then attaching a circle of fondant to the top, smoothing the sides and the top for a crisp edge. Trim the dowels. Lay the towers on a flat surface dusted with confectioner's sugar, seam-sides down. Dry overnight.

10 Roll out the remaining strengthened leaf-green fondant (used to cover the cake drum). Using the template, cut a wavy background pattern that will fit around the cake, with a gap at the front for the castle steps, and then loosely roll it up. Apply to the cake with a little water, using the cake drum to support the fondant roll as you unwind it and press it onto the cake.

pound cake (see p.231), filled and crumb-coated with buttercream (see p.29), 3in (7.5cm) tall

∗ 3lb 3oz (1.5kg) ivory fondant

∗ 5in (12.5cm) two-layer, vanilla sponge cake (see p.228), filled and crumb-coated with buttercream frosting, about 5in (12.5cm) in height

∗ 1 slab of pound cake (see p.231), 1in (2.5cm) thick

∗ ⅓ cup buttercream frosting

∗ 3oz (75g) each of 4–5 shades of green fondant, strengthened (see p.87)

∗ 2oz (50g) each of pink, fuchsia, yellow, lilac, brown, and red fondant, strengthened (see p.87)

∗ 1lb 2oz (500g) white fondant, strengthened (see p.87)

∗ 7oz (200g) fuchsia fondant, strengthened (see p.87)

∗ 1lb 2oz (500g) pink fondant, strengthened (see p.87)

∗ 10oz (300g) lilac fondant

For the garden

11 Use the template to cut shapes from the various shades of strengthened green fondant (reserve the darkest green for the trees), to create a patchwork effect of fields. Create striped fields by laying thin strips of pale fondant over darker fondant, and rolling them out together. Work around the cake, piecing together the field landscape neatly.

12 Roll out the pink, fuchsia, yellow, and lilac fondants, one at a time, and use the blossom plunger cutter to cut out lots of tiny blossoms. Provide each with a center of fondant in a contrasting color. Moisten the back of some flowers with a little water and attach to the cake. Put the others aside to decorate the board when the cake is finished.

13 Create trees by molding small trunks (about ⅔in/1.5cm high) and larger trunks (about ¾in/2cm high) from strengthened brown fondant. Scratch with a knife to look like bark, then moisten the reverse side, and fix to the cake. Roll out the darkest green fondant and use heart-shaped plunger cutters to create 2 sizes of treetops. Attach to the cake above the trunks. Cut out small hearts and circles from rolled red fondant, and attach to the treetops with a little water.

METHOD CONTINUES · · · ·

Princess mini cupcakes
Pipe cupcakes with buttercream frosting and top them with tiaras cut from thin strengthened fondant. Let dry and pipe beads on each tip. Paint them with silver dust. Secure the fondant hearts with water.

14 Roll out the white fondant, and cut out a cloud shape. It should be wide and long enough for the castle, including all 4 turrets, to sit comfortably on top, fanning out toward the steps at the front of the cake. Moisten the back of the cloud with a little water and attach to the top of the base cake. Smooth the edges to soften.

15 Form the remaining white fondant into a ball and then, using a knife, cut out a flight of stairs that will sit against the cake at the front. The stairs should be high enough to meet the trailing piece of cloud, about three-quarters of the way up the side of the cake. Cut a smaller cloud shape with the excess, and attach it to the covered cake drum, directly in the center. It should be wide enough for the princess to sit on top. Attach the stairs to the front of the cake with edible glue.

To bring all the elements together

16 Place 4 dowels into the base cake, using the 5in (12.5cm) cake base as a guide. Cut to height and place the ivory cake on top.

17 Place the towers around the cake as evenly as possible, using royal icing to secure the towers to the base cake and the sides of the ivory cake, ensuring that all the seams are facing inward. Press the dowels down into the base cake a little.

18 Roll out the ivory fondant on a cornstarch-dusted surface and cut out a rectangle shape that narrows slightly at one end. It should be a little more than 5in (12.5cm) in height and fit neatly onto the front of the cake to form the entrance. Fix into place with water.

19 Cut a heart-shaped door from the strengthened fuchsia fondant and score with vertical lines. Cut 2 tiny lilac hearts to make door handles and attach to the door. Attach the door to the cake with a little water. Roll out the strengthened yellow fondant and cut 4 small triangles to create the hinges. Attach to the sides of the door, and paint with gold dust mixed with grain alcohol. Roll out more fuchsia fondant on a cornstarch-dusted surface and cut 12 hearts using the plunger cutters: 4 small, 4 medium, and 4 large. Fix these to the towers with water to create windows.

20 Lift the dried roof from the cardboard cone and place on top of the central ivory cake, placing the seam at the back. Secure the roof with royal icing. Form a small ball of pink fondant and place it on the roof. Cut out 6 large fuchsia hearts, using the plunger cutter. Attach 1 to the front of the roof and another on top of the pink fondant ball on top. Model a fuchsia bow, and use water to attach it to the roof under the fondant ball.

Tip

Use pastillage, gum paste, or strengthened fondant instead of Mexican paste; these may, however, require extra time to dry thoroughly, ideally in a dry place such as a cupboard. You can use polystyrene cylinders instead of cake for the turrets.

21 Make 4 balls of pink fondant, each weighing about 2oz (50g). Dust your hands with cornstarch and form each into a cone-shaped roof, with the base of each cone just over 1¾in (4.5cm) in diameter. Attach to the top of each tower with royal icing. Top each turret with a fuchsia heart.

22 On a surface dusted with cornstarch, roll out the strengthened lilac fondant. Using the ribbon cutter, cut a ribbon about 1in (2.5cm) wide and 14in (35cm) long (trim to length when in place). Use a small circle cutter to create a crenellated top edge to the ribbon, and then attach it around the top of the ivory cake with a little water. Cut another piece of ribbon to fit over the entrance, with the crenellated top edge slightly wider than the base, and score the bottom of the ribbon with the back of a knife. Moisten and affix to the top of the entrance.

23 Use a wavy attachment on the ribbon cutter to create the crenellated top edge of the ribbons that will top the towers, and a sharp knife to cut the bottom edge. Cut 4 ribbons in this way, each about ½in (1cm) wide and 7in (17cm) long, and attach to the top of the towers, where they meet the roofs.

24 Cover the seam at the back of the main roof with a row of tiny hearts, cut from fuchsia fondant and applied with water.

25 Position the princess on the cloud shape on the cake drum, in front of the steps, using royal icing to secure. Dot the remaining blossoms around the board, moistening the backs with a little water to adhere. Trim the cake drum with pink ribbon, securing it with a little craft glue and making sure the seam is at the back.

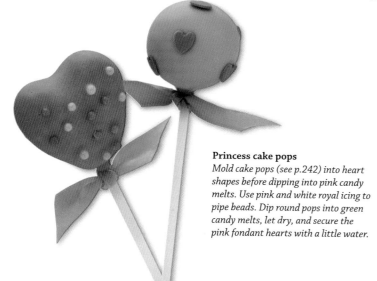

Princess cake pops
Mold cake pops (see p.242) into heart shapes before dipping into pink candy melts. Use pink and white royal icing to pipe beads. Dip round pops into green candy melts, let dry, and secure the pink fondant hearts with a little water.

Pirate ship cake

Set sail on the seven seas with a spectacular pirate ship, complete with an anchor and skull-and-crossbones sails. Displayed on a fondant wave-encrusted board, this cake is carved from layers of sponge cake and covered with weather-beaten fondant planks.

TIMING allow 1½ days, including drying time

 SERVES 40

Equipment

* fondant roller
* multi-ribbon cutter
* circle cutters: 1in (2.5cm), ¾in (2cm), and 1¼in (3cm)
* frilling tool
* 1 wooden dowel
* 2 wooden skewers
* anchor cutter
* 14in (35cm) round cake drum
* white rice paper
* skull-and-crossbones stencil
* 3ft (1m) navy satin ribbon (½in/1cm wide)

1 A day before you wish to serve, halve your cake so that you have two 5in x 10in (12.5cm x 25cm) pieces, each 3in (7.5cm) thick. Carefully cut 1 of these pieces into 2 layers, each 5in x 10in x 1½in (12.5cm x 25cm x 4cm). Sandwich 1 of the thin layers on top of the thicker piece of cake with buttercream frosting. Take the remaining layer of cake and cut it into 3 equal pieces, 3in (8cm) long and 5in (12.5cm) wide. Sandwich 2 of these together with buttercream frosting and fix to one end of the cake with more buttercream frosting to make the bow of the ship. Stick the remaining piece of cake to the other end of the cake with buttercream frosting, to become the stern. Place the whole cake in the freezer for 30–60 minutes, or until just firm.

2 Carve the bow of the ship into a prow-shaped point, using a sharp serrated knife. Carve the sides into a smooth curve toward the back of the ship, and from the top of the deck down to the base with a gentle slope. Carve the steps from the tallest area of the cake for the stern of the ship, using a ruler to ensure that they are level and evenly spaced. Crumb-coat the entire cake with buttercream frosting (see p.29), and let set for 30 minutes.

METHOD CONTINUES • • • •

BRING IT ALL TOGETHER

Carving and covering cakes *see p.65*

Using multi-ribbon cutters *see p.118*

Using cookie cutters *see pp.106–07*

Ingredients

* 10in (25cm) square
  pound cake (see p.231),
  about 3in (7.5cm) deep
* 1lb 5oz (600g)
  buttercream frosting
  (see pp.24–25)
* cornstarch, for dusting
* 1lb 5oz (600g)
  brown fondant
* 2oz (50g) black fondant
* 2oz (50g) red fondant,
  strengthened (see p.87)
* 3½oz (100g) gold fondant,
  strengthened (see p.87)
* dark brown
  coloring paste
* 1oz (25g) gray fondant,
  strengthened (see p.87)
* 9oz (250g) blue fondant
  and 5½oz (150g) white
  fondant, marbled (see p.47)
* superwhite icing whitener
* blue coloring paste
* 2oz (50g) brown
  gum paste
* edible black felt-tip pen
* gold and silver
  luster dusts
* grain alcohol
  or vodka

3 Dust a flat surface with cornstarch, and roll out some brown fondant to ⅙in (4mm) thick. Use this to cover the top of the ship, including the decks and the stairs. Use a sharp knife to score the surface with long and short floorboards, about 1in (2.5cm). Use your knife to scratch lines and swirls.

4 Roll out the remaining brown fondant, and use the ribbon cutter to cut strips about 1in (2.5cm) wide, in many different lengths. Lightly moisten the back of the strips and place them around the base of the ship, continuing upward until two-thirds of the ship is covered. Score the surface of the strips with a sharp knife. Use a toothpick to poke all 4 corners of each strip to create nail holes.

5 Use the 1in (2.5cm) circle cutter to cut 3 portholes from each side of the ship, below where the wooden strips end. Remove the cake and fondant and discard. On a cornstarch-dusted surface, roll out the black fondant to ¹⁄₁₆in (2mm) thick and cut 6 circles with the same cutter. Moisten the backs of each and insert into the holes created in the ship.

6 Roll out the strengthened red fondant on a cornstarch-dusted surface. Cut 6 circles, using the 1¼in (3cm) cutter, and then cut the center out with the 1in (2.5cm) cutter. Let set for 15 minutes and then moisten the back and attach to the cake so that the red circles frame the portholes.

7 Next, roll out the gold fondant on a surface dusted with cornstarch. Cut panels to fit the sides and back of the ship, from the paneled brown fondant to the top of the deck, adding about ¼in (5mm) so that it sticks up above the deck a little. You will need 2 panels for the prow, 2 for the lower deck in the center, 2 that are cut to fit the shape of the stairs, and 1 for the back of the ship. Use the point of the frilling tool to poke holes in the surface of the fondant, to resemble rivets.

8 Press the dowel into the center of the ship, with 2 skewers on each side. Cut to height of sails (see step 12). Mix brown coloring paste with water and paint the skewers. Roll out the gray fondant on a cornstarch-dusted surface and use the cutter for an anchor. Let dry for 3 hours.

9 On a cornstarch-dusted surface, roll out the marbled blue-and-white fondant to ¼in (6mm) and cover the cake drum. Place the ship on its center. Pinch the marbled fondant to create waves over the surface surrounding the ship. Paint the tops of the waves with superwhite icing whitener, and the base with blue coloring paste mixed with water.

Tip
Dilute brown coloring paste with water or grain alcohol and wash the boards of the ship on both the sides and the deck. The streaks of light brown diluted paste help it to look more realistic and sea-worn.

10 Roll out a long rope of brown gum paste, about ¼in (5mm) wide, and cut into 18 segments about 1¼in (3cm) long. Let dry for 30 minutes and then moisten the ends with water and fix to the front and rear decks to create spindles for the bannister. Measure the length of each bannister and cut out strips of brown gum paste, wider than the spindles. Let dry. Fix to the spindles with some water.

11 Using the ¾in (2cm) circle cutter, cut 2 cannon holes from each side of the ship, at the rear, on the gold panels (see opposite) and replace the centers with black fondant circles, as you did in step 5. Roll out the red fondant and cut circular frames to fit around the cannon holes, using the biggest and medium circle cutters. Fix around the holes with water. Cut strips of red fondant, ¹⁄₁₆in (2mm) wide. Moisten the back and fit around the top of the gold panel, to trim. Add rivets to the trim with a frilling tool.

12 Cut the rice paper into a variety of different-sized squares. On the largest sail, place the skull-and-crossbones stencil and use the black felt-tip edible pen to paint on the image. Cut holes from the center of the base and the top of each sail, then slide them onto the skewers and the dowel. Take 3 pea-sized balls of brown gum paste and press them down into flat circles. Moisten the base of each circle and place on top of the skewers and wooden dowel.

13 Mix some gold luster dust with grain alcohol and paint the gold panels. Moisten the back of the dried anchor and attach it to the side of the boat, near the front. Mix some silver luster dust with grain alcohol and paint the anchor. Trim the cake drum with the ribbon, making sure the join is at the back.

Pirate cake pops
Dip cake pops (see pp.242–43) into melted peach candy melts and decorate with gum-paste eye patches and bandanas. Use a piping tip to cut out white gum-paste circles, and fix them to the top with edible glue. Use edible pens for other details. You can form cake crumbs into a parrot shape, dip them into melted green candy melts, and add fondant eyes, a beak, and 3-color wings, scored with a veining tool.

Soccer ball cake

Decorating this cake is like creating a patchwork quilt. You have to line up the edges of each fondant shape carefully before attaching it to the cake. Although time-consuming to prepare, this cake and the football cake (see p.182) will be the crowning glory for anyone who loves sports.

 TIMING allow 3–4 days, including drying time

 **SERVES** 20

Equipment

* 13in (33cm) cake drum
* fondant roller
* multi-ribbon cutter, straight edges
* fondant smoother
* large hexagon and pentagon cutters
* 3ft (1m) black satin ribbon (½in/1cm wide)
* craft glue

Ingredients

* 7oz (200g) green fondant, strengthened (see p.87)
* 7oz (200g) white fondant, strengthened (see p.87)
* cornstarch, for dusting
* edible glue
* 6in (15cm) pound ball cake (see p.237)
* ⅔ cup buttercream
* confectioner's sugar
* 1lb 5oz (600g) white fondant
* 7oz (200g) black fondant

1 Three to four days before you decorate the cake, cover the cake drum (see p.51), using the ribbon cutter to cut strips of both green and white strengthened fondant, rolled out to about ⅛in (3mm) thick on a surface dusted with cornstarch. Brush the cake drum with edible glue and place alternating colors on top. Smooth down over the edges and surface with the fondant smoother, and cut off any excess. Set aside to dry.

2 Place the ball cake on a flat surface and crumb-coat it with buttercream frosting (see p.29). Let it set for 1 hour, then spread another thin layer of buttercream frosting over the surface of the cake, until smooth. On separate surfaces that have been dusted with confectioner's sugar, roll out the black and white fondant to ⅛in (3mm), making sure they are the same thickness.

3 Using the cutters, cut out 5 white hexagons and 5 black pentagons at a time, keeping them covered with plastic wrap while you work. Cover up the excess fondant. Place a black pentagon on the top center of the ball, securing it into place with a little extra buttercream frosting. Encircle with 5 white hexagons, making sure that the edges meet neatly.

4 Roll out more hexagons and pentagons, and add them to the surface of the ball to create the classic pattern. Gradually build up the shapes to cover the whole ball, turning it over when you have covered the top half. The shapes may need to be molded to ensure that they fit together. Recut any shapes if necessary.

5 When the cake is complete, let dry overnight. Carefully move it to the covered cake drum. Secure with buttercream frosting. Attach the satin ribbon around the base of the covered cake drum with craft glue. Make sure the seam is at the back.

Tips

When carving the football cake (see p.182), it helps to have a photograph in front of you. Better still, print out a ball template (see p.245), place it on top of the cake, and then cut the outline using small, even cuts with a serrated knife.

BRING IT ALL TOGETHER

Covering a cake drum *see p.51*

Using a molded cake pan *see p.237*

Carving and covering cakes *see p.65*

Football cake

This hand-carved cake (see p.181) is covered in fondant and stitched with a quilting tool. Finish the cake drum with a black ribbon (see p.180).

FOOTBALL CAKE **VARIATION:** BALL GAME MINI CAKES *p.183*

TIMING allow 3 days, including drying time

SERVES 20

Equipment

* 13in (33cm) round cake drum
* football template (see p.245)
* fondant roller
* fondant smoother
* stitching (quilting) tool
* multi-ribbon cutter, straight edges

Ingredients

* 7oz (200g) green fondant, strengthened (see p.87)
* 10oz (300g) white fondant, strengthened (see p.87)
* 10in (25cm) two-layer pound cake, sandwiched with buttercream
* ⅔ cup buttercream
* confectioner's sugar
* 2lb 2oz (1kg) brown fondant
* cornstarch, for dusting

1 Three days before the celebration, cover the cake drum (see p.180, step 1), and set aside to dry. Freeze the cake and place it on a flat surface. Using a sharp, serrated knife and the template, carve in the shape of a football. Once carved, crumb-coat with a little buttercream frosting and allow to settle for 1 hour. Smooth another thin coat of buttercream frosting over the crumb-coated surface. Refrigerate to firm, for about 1 hour.

2 Place on a firm surface and neaten with a sharp knife. Moisten the cake's surface with water on a pastry brush. Dust a flat surface with confectioner's sugar, and roll out the brown fondant to ¼in (5mm) thick and large enough to wrap around the cake. Lift onto the ball and smooth with your hands.

3 Gather the fondant together under the points at each end of the ball. Trim any excess. Rub cornstarch onto the cut marks, making sure they remain on the underside of the ball. Smooth down with the fondant smoother. Using the stitching tool, mark 4 evenly spaced horizontal seams on the ball, from one pointed end to the other, making sure not to score through to the cake.

4 Roll out the remaining white fondant on a surface dusted with cornstarch to ¹⁄₁₆in (2mm) thick, and use the ribbon cutter to cut out strips long enough to wrap around the ball. Cut a single thin strip for the central stitching on the ball and 8 smaller strips to fix onto this. Use a little water to attach.

5 Move the cake onto the covered cake drum, and secure with buttercream icing. Finish the board with a ribbon (see p.180).

FOOTBALL CAKE **VARIATION**

Ball game mini cakes

Celebrate sport with some cute mini cakes, each adorned with a stenciled ball on top. You can top them with virtually any type of ball to please the crowd. You can use a scraper to help remove excess frosting when you are stenciling the cakes. Follow more tips on stenciling on pp.125–31.

 TIMING 2½ hrs   **MAKES** 12

Equipment

* fondant roller
* circle cutters, 6in (15cm) and 2in (5cm) diameter
* 12 x 3in (7.5cm) round cake boards
* fondant smoother
* 3 x sports ball stencils
* 6ft (2m) black ribbon, ⅔in (1.5cm) wide

Ingredients

* confectioner's sugar
* 4lb 8oz (2kg) white fondant
* 12 mini pound cakes (see p.231), 2in (5cm) wide and 1⅓in (3.5cm) high, crumb-coated with buttercream (see p.29)
* tylose powder
* ½ cup royal icing (see p.34), in black, red, and white
* 2oz (50g) orange fondant, strengthened (see p.87)

1 On a surface dusted with confectioner's sugar, roll out the white fondant to ¼in (5mm) thick. Use the large cutter to cut 12 circles and cover each crumb-coated cake. Trim off any excess. Dot buttercream frosting on each cake board. Place the covered cakes on top. Use the fondant smoother to shape the tops.

2 Strengthen the remaining white fondant with tylose powder (see p.87), and roll it to ⅛in (3mm) thick. Use a knife to cut out 8 squares, 2¼in (6cm) in size. Place the soccer ball stencil on one and spread black royal icing over the top. Peel off the stencil and repeat on 3 more squares. Stencil 4 baseballs using the red royal icing. Cut out 4 squares from orange fondant rolled to the same thickness, and stencil white icing basketballs on top.

3 Use the smaller cutter to cut a disk around each ball. Dab each cake with a little water, and carefully place a design on each. Trim the cakes with ribbon secured with royal icing.

Butterflies and blossoms

These charming cupcakes are spread with rich vanilla buttercream frosting, topped with pretty pink fondant butterflies, and nestled in delicate lace paper liners. Serve alongside delightful piped peach cupcakes with a simple yet elegant blossom on top.

TIMING allow 1½ days, including drying time   **MAKES** 12

Equipment

* fondant roller
* butterfly plunger cutters, medium and small
* blossom plunger cutter, medium
* piping bag with large open star tip (such as Wilton no. 1M)
* lace paper liners

Ingredients

* cornstarch, for dusting
* 7oz (200g) pink fondant, strengthened (see p.87)
* 7oz (200g) white fondant, strengthened (see p.87)
* 12 cupcakes (see p.240)
* 2lb 2oz (1kg) buttercream frosting (see p.24), half colored with peach coloring paste (see pp.24–25)

1 A day before you wish to serve the cupcakes, on a flat surface dusted with cornstarch, roll out the strengthened pink fondant to about ¹⁄₁₆in (1mm) thick. Use plunger cutters to cut out 10 medium and 10 small butterflies. Bend gently in the center, and place along the crease of an open book lined with parchment paper to dry in shape overnight.

2 Roll out the strengthened white fondant on a surface dusted with cornstarch to about ¹⁄₁₆in (1mm) thick, and use the blossom plunger cutter to cut out 10 blossoms. Place on parchment paper to dry overnight.

3 Using the cone method (see p.33), fill the cooled cupcakes with buttercream frosting. Using a palette knife, spread uncolored buttercream frosting on 6 cupcakes.

4 Fill the piping bag with peach buttercream frosting and attach the open star tip. Pipe the remaining cupcakes.

5 Moisten the back of each dried blossom with water and press gently onto the piped cupcakes. Moisten the back of each butterfly and press onto the surface of the smooth-frosted cupcakes. Slip the cupcakes into the lace paper liners and arrange on a stand.

BRING IT ALL TOGETHER

Using plunger cutters
see pp.101–03

Filling cupcakes
see p.33

Piping cupcakes
see p.32

Halloween pumpkin cake

This spooky jack-o'-lantern cake is carved from a rich pound cake covered in orange fondant and carefully scored to resemble a real Halloween pumpkin. Cover the cake drum with purple strengthened fondant at least a day before you start decorating.

HALLOWEEN PUMPKIN CAKE **VARIATION:** SCARY CAKE POPS *p.189*

 **TIMING** allow ½ day, including drying time

SERVES 25

Equipment

* fondant roller
* star plunger cutter
* 13in (33cm) purple fondant-covered round cake drum
* veining tool
* set of triangle cutters
* ball tool
* skewers
* 3ft (1m) black satin ribbon (½in/1cm wide)
* craft glue

1 On a surface dusted with cornstarch, roll out the gold fondant to about ¹⁄₁₆in (1mm) thick, and cut out about 12 stars using the plunger cutter. Moisten the back of each star with water and stick them onto the covered cake drum with edible glue. Set aside to dry.

2 On a surface dusted with cornstarch, knead the orange fondant and form into 6 sausage shapes that are long enough to extend from the top of the cake to the base, and about 2in (5cm) wide. Moisten the backs of the sausages and press them onto the sides of the crumb-coated ball cake at even intervals, to add definition and build up the shape.

3 Roll out the remaining orange fondant to about ⅙in (4mm) thick, so it is large enough to cover the ball and the sausage-shaped fondant detailing. Cover the ball, pushing the fondant into the grooves between the sausages. Dust your hands with

METHOD CONTINUES · · · ·

BRING IT ALL TOGETHER

Using a molded cake pan *see p.237*

Using cookie cutters *see pp.106–07*

Using petal dusts *see p.136*

Ingredients

* cornstarch, for dusting
* 2oz (50g) gold fondant, strengthened (see p.87)
* edible glue
* 1lb 8oz (700g) orange fondant
* 6in (15cm) pound ball cake (see p.231), leveled and crumb-coated with buttercream frosting (see p.29)
* 2oz (50g) black fondant
* 2oz (50g) green fondant, strengthened (see p.87)
* gold luster dust

Tips

If you cannot purchase fondant in the desired colors, use food coloring paste, bearing in mind that the final shade will be darker once the color has set. You can use leftover fondant to create tiny pumpkins to decorate the table.

cornstarch to smooth down further. Gather the fondant around the base of the cake and cut off any excess, smoothing down. Move the cake to the covered cake drum.

4 Use the veining tool to score the surface of the pumpkin; work in a downward motion. Use the triangle cutters to cut out eyes and a nose from the front of the pumpkin and carefully remove the fondant. Use a sharp knife to cut out a mouth shape, and remove the fondant.

5 On a surface dusted with cornstarch, roll out the black fondant to about 1/16in (2mm) thick, and cut out triangles and a mouth shape, the same size as the shapes on the pumpkin. Moisten the backs of each with a little water and press into the cutouts on the pumpkin. Smooth down with your fingers.

6 To model the stalk, form a ball of strengthened green fondant and roll into a thick sausage with your hands. Press it down onto a hard surface dusted with cornstarch so that the top is flattened and the bottom begins to fan out. Use a ball tool to smooth out the bottom edges and expand them outward. Use a veining tool to score the surface.

7 Cut a circle from the orange fondant at the top of the pumpkin. Moisten the base of the stalk and press into place in the circle. Use the veining tool and/or the ball tool to press the orange fondant upward, over the edges of the base of the stalk so it looks realistic.

8 Roll out thin ropes of strengthened green fondant and cut to different lengths. Dust the skewers with a little cornstarch. Wrap the ropes of green fondant around the skewers; let them set for 10 minutes while they start to set and hold their shape. Remove from the skewers and attach to the pumpkin stalk and the board with a little water.

9 Dust the stars with a little gold luster dust. Attach the ribbon around the base of the cake drum with a little craft glue, placing the seam at the back.

HALLOWEEN PUMPKIN CAKE **VARIATION**

Scary cake pops

These festive lanterns, spooky black cats, and witches' hat-cake pops are ideal treats for a Halloween party. Make a few batches to delight trick-or-treaters and stand them upright for a striking centerpiece. When modeling your shapes, be sure to wrap excess fondant in plastic wrap for future use.

 TIMING allow 1 day, including drying time

MAKES 24

Equipment

* fondant roller
* circle cutter, 2in (5cm)
* 24 cake-pop sticks

Ingredients

* 1oz (25g) yellow fondant
* green coloring paste
* tylose powder
* cornstarch, for dusting
* 3½oz (100g) black fondant, strengthened
* 24 un-dipped cake pops on sticks (see pp.242–43), 8 formed into cones with a flat base (for hats), and 8 with vertical ridges (for pumpkins)
* 14oz (400g) black candy melts
* 7oz (200g) orange candy melts
* edible black pen
* 1oz (25g) pink fondant

1 Color a little yellow fondant with coloring paste, strengthen (see p.87), and mold into 8 stalks. Roll out the black fondant, use the cutter to cut 8 circles, and then poke a central hole through each and place on scrunched foil. Allow all shapes to dry overnight.

2 Dip the hat (cone) and cat (round) cake pops into the melted black candy melts and set aside, upright, to harden. Dip the pumpkins into the melted orange melts and top with the stalks.

3 Roll out the remaining black fondant, then cut out the pumpkin features. Cut triangles for the cats' ears and strips to wrap around the hats. Let dry for 20 minutes. Use the yellow fondant and the pink fondant to create features for the cats, adding details to the cats' eyes with edible pen. Attach all of the cat and pumpkin features onto the pops with a little water.

4 Moisten the black circles, then slide them onto the hat cake-pop sticks. Moisten the black strips and fix to each hat.

Teddy bear mini cakes

These colorful cakes are layered with fondant and gum paste, then piped to create building blocks—perfect for a baby shower, newborn celebration, or an all-important first birthday. The shade of the colored royal icing will deepen with time, so aim for one shade lighter.

TIMING allow 1½ hours **MAKES** 10

Equipment

* fondant roller
* square cutters: 2¾in (7cm) and 2in (5cm)
* fondant smoother
* mini bear cutter
* piping bag with tips (such as PME no. 1 and no. 5)

Ingredients

* 3lb 3oz (1.5kg) white fondant
* cornstarch, for dusting
* 10 x 2¾in (7cm) square mini cakes, halved and filled with buttercream frosting, crumb-coated with ganache (see p.29)
* 7oz (200g) each orange, lilac, blue, green, and pink fondant
* edible glue
* ¾ cup royal icing, for piping (see p.35)
* black, orange, lilac, blue, green, and pink coloring pastes

1 Knead the white fondant until it is soft, and roll out a large circle on a cornstarch-dusted surface, to ⅛in (3mm) thick. Cut the fondant into 12 squares to cover the cakes. Lay a square of fondant on each cake, and smooth it down over the sides with a fondant smoother. Trim off excess and let set for 30 minutes.

2 On a cornstarch-dusted surface, roll out the orange fondant to ¹⁄₁₆in (2mm) thick. Cut out 10 squares with the large square cutter. Place the small cutter in the center of each square and cut, leaving the outline. Let dry for 5 minutes, then lift them onto parchment paper. Cut out 4 teddy bears and place alongside. Repeat with the lilac, blue, green, and pink fondant, so you have 10 square outlines and 4 teddy bears in each color.

3 When the outlines are starting to firm, brush each with a little edible glue and press onto 5 sides of the cakes (leaving the base as it is). Press the edges together. Roll 20 tiny balls of white fondant with your hands, and press into circles. Moisten and fix to the faces of the teddy bears to make their snouts.

4 Color a small amount of royal icing with black coloring paste. Fit a no. 1 tip to a piping bag and fill. Pipe details onto each of the teddy bears. Set aside to dry.

5 Divide the remaining royal icing among 5 bowls and tint each with coloring paste to match the fondant shades. Attach a no. 5 tip to a piping bag and fill with a shade of icing. Pipe a number or letter on 3 sides of each cake, piping the outline first and then filling in the inside.

6 Moisten the reverse of each teddy bear with a little water and attach to the remaining 2 sides of each cake, making sure that the colors match.

Tip

If you are not confident at piping freehand, you can use letter and number cutters to emboss the surface of the squares and pipe to fill them in later. Alternatively, cut them out from the appropriate fondant and fix them in place with edible glue.

BRING IT ALL TOGETHER

Using cookie cutters
see pp.106–07

Basic royal icing piping *see p.75*

Newborn celebration cake

This elegant cake is ideal for baby showers, newborn celebrations, and formal christenings. Tiny piped beads and dots highlight the fondant heart and ribbons, while swags, hearts, and buttons add beautiful, symmetrical detail. A template makes it easy to create perfect shapes.

TIMING allow 1½ days, including drying time    **SERVES** 10

Equipment

* 11in (28cm) cake drum
* fondant roller
* multi-ribbon cutter, wavy edge
* stitching (quilting) tool
* set of circle cutters
* piping bag and tips (such as PME no. 1, 2, and 3)
* heart plunger cutters
* heart template (see p.244)
* 3ft (1m) yellow ribbon
* craft glue

Ingredients

* 2lb 2oz (1kg) white fondant
* tylose powder
* confectioner's sugar
* 2lb 2oz (1kg) yellow fondant, strengthened (see p.87)
* edible glue
* 8in (20cm) lemon sponge cake (see p.229), with lemon buttercream
* ½ cup royal icing, for piping (see p.35)

1 A day before you serve the cake, strengthen the white fondant (see p.87) and use it to cover the cake drum (see p.51). Roll out the yellow fondant on a confectioner's-sugar dusted surface to ¼in (5mm) thick and use it to cover the cake (see p.50). Wrap both colors in plastic wrap. Dry overnight.

2 Roll out the white fondant to ⅛in (3mm) thick. Using the multi-ribbon cutter, cut 16 wavy ribbons 1¼in x 3in (3cm x 7.5cm). Mark out 16 evenly spaced vertical lines around the side of the cake. Attach the ribbons to the marks with edible glue. Use the stitching tool to emboss vertical stitch marks on the ribbons.

3 Roll out a large piece of white fondant thinly and cut 8 rectangles (3½in x 3¼in/9cm x 8cm). Create swags with 2 horizontal pleats, pinching the edges. Adjust so the swags neatly span 3 ribbons. Brush each end with a little water, and attach to the cake. Roll out more white fondant, and cut out 9 small circles with a cutter. Use a slightly smaller cutter to emboss each "button." Use a no. 3 piping tip to cut out 2 holes in the center of each. Affix to the cake where the swags meet, reserving 1 for later (see step 5).

4 Roll out the yellow fondant and cut 8 small and 8 medium hearts, using plunger cutters. Affix to the cake. Roll out more white fondant, and cut around the heart template. Attach it to the top of the cake with diluted edible glue. Roll out the remaining yellow fondant, and cut out the baby feet. Stick on the fondant heart, and stitch around the edge with the stitching tool.

5 Fit the piping bag with a no. 1 tip. Pipe a line of royal icing picot dots around the heart. "Thread" each button. Pipe beads around the base of the cake, using a no. 2 tip. Fix the ribbon around the drum with craft glue. Cover the seam with a button.

BRING IT ALL TOGETHER

Using multi-ribbon cutters *see p.118*

Modeling embellishments *see p.96*

Piping dots, beads, and flowers *see p.80*

Gingerbread house

With its intricate piping and fondant cutout detail, this impressive gingerbread house is sure to please a crowd and provide a whimsical backdrop for your Christmas celebrations. Bake the gingerbread pieces in batches, and, once cool, use a serrated knife to refine the shapes.

TIMING allow 2 days, including drying time

 MAKES 1 gingerbread house

Equipment

* rolling pin
* gingerbread house template (see p.246)
* square, Christmas tree, heart, and circle cookie cutters
* fondant smoother
* piping bag
* round piping tips (such as PME no. 1, 2, and 3)
* 11in (28cm) white fondant-covered square cake drum (see p.51)
* 3ft (1m) red satin ribbon (½in/1cm wide)
* craft glue

Ingredients

* 1 batch gingerbread dough (see p.235)
* 1½ cups royal icing, piping consistency (see p.35)
* 3½oz (100g) red fondant, strengthened (see p.87)
* cornstarch, for dusting

1 Roll out the dough on a floured sheet of parchment paper, to about ¼in (5mm) thick. Using the template, cut out the pieces, including a spare panel (see Tips, opposite). Use cutters to cut out windows and trees.

2 Transfer the gingerbread and parchment paper to a baking sheet. Bake in an oven preheated to 350°F (180°C), until golden. Cool on the baking sheet. Move to a wire rack to cool.

3 Attach a no. 2 tip to a piping bag, and fill it with royal icing. Pipe tiles onto each roof panel in a series of loops. Change to a no. 1 tip, and pipe patterns and picot dots (see p.80) on the walls and the front of the house. Outline the windows and door, and pipe the surface of the chimney. Pipe an outline on the trees. Allow each piece to dry before assembling.

4 Assemble the house (see pp.66–67). Put the chimney together, then attach it to the house. Use the spare panel to cut a ½in- (1cm-) wide strip, as long as the roof, to run along the top. Glue to the rooftop with royal icing.

5 Roll out the red fondant on a cornstarch-dusted surface. Use cutters for tiny hearts, circles, and a wreath on the door. Roll small balls with your hands. Let everything dry overnight. When dry, use a no. 1 tip to pipe royal icing onto the wreath in dots.

6 Switch to a no. 3 tip, and decorate the seams with piped beading (see p.80). Glue the fondant shapes to the house with royal icing and allow it to harden for 24 hours. Once dry, lift the house and dot the underside of the walls with royal icing. Place on the covered drum, and pipe a snail trail at the bottom. Attach the ribbon around the drum (see Tips, opposite).

Tips

Bake an extra roof panel, which can be cut down for supports and the ridge line on the top of the roof. Glue the ribbon around the drum with craft glue, taking care to put the seam at the back. Cover the seam with a dot of royal icing.

BRING IT ALL TOGETHER

Making a template
see p.57

Basic royal icing piping *see p.75*

Building with ginger-bread *see pp.66–67*

Using cookie cutters
see pp.106–07

Shades of pink

This spectacular shaded cake (also known as an ombré cake) is surprisingly easy to make. Gradated shades of pink cake are sandwiched together with buttercream, and the cake is frosted to match, with two pretty pink fondant butterflies resting on top.

 TIMING allow 1½ days, including drying time

 SERVES 20 finger portions; 10 for dessert

Equipment

* 5 x 6in (15cm) round cake pans, greased and lined (see p.236)
* 6in (15cm) cake board
* turntable or lazy Susan
* scraper, smooth-edged
* butterfly plunger cutters in 2 sizes

Ingredients

* butter, for greasing
* 1½ batches of classic vanilla sponge cake batter (see p.228)
* large tub of dark-pink (fuchsia) coloring paste
* 3 cups (1 batch) vanilla buttercream frosting (see p.24)
* 1oz (25g) dark-pink fondant, strengthened (see p.87)

1 A day before you wish to serve, bake the cake. Preheat the oven to 350°F (180°C). Divide the cake batter between 5 bowls. Add ⅛ teaspoon of pink coloring paste to the first bowl; ¼ teaspoon to the second; ½ teaspoon to the third; ¾ teaspoon to the fourth; and 1 teaspoon to the final bowl. Mix all bowls well, until the batter is evenly colored.

2 Pour the batter into the cake pans and bake for 20 minutes, test, and cool (see p.238). Level the cakes (see p.239). Spread a little buttercream frosting onto the cake board, place the darkest cake on top, and move to the turntable.

3 Layer the cakes with buttercream frosting (see p.28), starting with the darkest at the bottom to the lightest at the top. Crumb-coat the cake (see p.29), and let rest for 1 hour.

4 Separate the remaining buttercream frosting into 5 bowls and add the pink coloring paste to create 5 shades of frosting, from light to dark. Starting with the darkest shade of buttercream, frost the base up to about 1in (2.5cm). Continue up the cake using the remaining shades of buttercream frosting, from dark to light, until the sides are covered. Frost the top with the lightest shade.

5 Pull the scraper across the side of the cake as you turn the turntable. Push a palette knife into the buttercream frosting and spin the turntable, to create lines where the color changes.

6 On a surface dusted with cornstarch, roll out the dark-pink fondant to ¹⁄₁₆in (2mm) thick. Using a plunger cutter, cut out 2 butterflies and rest them in an open book, on a sheet of parchment paper. Dry overnight. Attach the butterflies to the top of the cake with a little buttercream.

BRING IT ALL TOGETHER

Filling a layer cake
see p.28

Crumb-coating a cake
see p.29

Using plunger cutters
see pp.101-03

Cupcake bouquet

Pipe a medley of cupcakes to create buttercream roses, and arrange them in a ceramic flowerpot to create a delightful centerpiece for any occasion. You could choose a larger pot to feed a crowd. While piping can take time to master, the end result is well worth the effort.

CUPCAKE BOUQUET **VARIATION:** HEART-SHAPED POSY CAKE *pp.200-01*

 TIMING 1½ hrs   **MAKES** 12

Equipment

* large piping bag with injector tip, or plain round tip (see p.74)
* large flower drop tip (such as Wilton no. 2D)
* Styrofoam ball, about 4in (10cm) wide
* ceramic flowerpot, about 5in (12.5cm) wide
* decorative ribbon

Ingredients

* 12 cupcakes (see p.240)
* ⅓ cup buttercream frosting (see pp.24–25)
* ⅓ cup buttercream frosting, colored pale pink
* ⅓ cup buttercream frosting, colored fuchsia
* 1 tbsp royal icing (see p.34)

1 When the cupcakes have cooled, fill each cake with a little buttercream frosting, using a large round tip or an injector tip on a large piping bag.

2 Fix a large flower drop tip to the same piping bag, and pipe a rose on 4 cupcakes. Start from the center of the cupcake and swirl outward in a counterclockwise direction, using even pressure, until the entire surface of the cupcake is covered with a piped rose.

3 Wash the piping bag or fit the same tip to a new piping bag, and fill the bag with pale pink buttercream frosting. Pipe 4 more cupcakes, using the same technique. Pipe the remaining cupcakes with fuchsia buttercream frosting in the same way. Allow the cupcakes to set for 15 minutes.

4 Place the Styrofoam ball into the flowerpot and press 6 toothpicks into the surface, about 3½in (9cm) apart. Spread a little royal icing on the base of a cupcake liner, and press it firmly onto a toothpick that has been inserted into the ball. Hold in place for 30 seconds, until the icing begins to dry. Repeat for the next cupcake in the same color, and then attach 2 cupcakes of each color.

5 Wrap the flowerpot with decorative ribbon tied into a pretty bow. Place the remaining cupcakes around the flowerpot.

BRING IT ALL TOGETHER

Filling cupcakes
see p.33

Piping a buttercream rose *see p.79*

BRING IT ALL TOGETHER

Covering a cake drum
see p.51

Piping a buttercream rose *see p.79*

CUPCAKE BOUQUET **VARIATION**

Heart-shaped posy cake

Celebrate a special occasion, such as an anniversary or Valentine's day, with an elegant heart cake, extravagantly piped with lilac buttercream frosting roses to create a flurry of flowers. For best results, start piping as soon as you've frosted your cake, to ensure that your flowers adhere to the surface.

 TIMING allow 1½ days, including drying time

 **SERVES** 15

Equipment

* fondant roller
* 12in (30cm) heart-shaped cake drum
* fondant smoother
* piping bag
* large drop flower tip (such as Wilton no. 2D)
* 3ft (1m) soft green satin ribbon (½in/1cm wide)
* craft glue

Ingredients

* cornstarch, for dusting
* 9oz (250g) white fondant, strengthened (see p.87)
* 8in (20cm) two-layer, heart-shaped vanilla sponge cake, filled and crumb-coated (see p.29) with buttercream frosting
* 1½ cups buttercream frosting, colored with lilac coloring paste

1 A day before you want to serve the cake, on a flat surface dusted with cornstarch, roll out the strengthened white fondant to ¹⁄₁₆in (2mm) thick and cover the heart-shaped cake drum using a fondant smoother. Set aside to dry overnight.

2 Place the crumb-coated cake on a flat surface and fill a piping bag, fitted with a large drop flower tip, with lilac-colored buttercream frosting.

3 Starting on the top of the cake, pipe a series of roses with the buttercream frosting, starting from the middle of a rose and applying even pressure as you pipe in a counterclockwise direction. Each rose should measure about ¾in (2cm) in diameter.

4 Continue across the entire surface of the cake and the sides, until you have covered it completely. Fill any spaces between the roses with small piped buttercream stars.

5 Using a large, wide spatula, lift the cake onto the covered cake drum. Fix the ribbon around the base of the cake drum with craft glue, making sure that the seam is at the back.

Handbag cake

This whimsical designer-bag cake, with its quilted flap and metallic chain, is incredibly realistic and easier to make than it looks. Use a veining tool to create authentic detail on the sides and main body.

 TIMING allow 1½ days, including drying time

 SERVES 40 finger portions

Equipment

* ✳ fondant roller
* ✳ fondant smoother
* ✳ veining tool
* ✳ 13in (33cm) fondant-covered cake drum
* ✳ 8in (20cm) round cake board or pan, to use as a template
* ✳ stitching (quilting) tool
* ✳ wide round piping tip (such as PME no. 4)
* ✳ 3ft (1m) white satin ribbon (½in/1cm wide)
* ✳ craft glue

1 Halve the square sponge cake across the center, and spread the top of one half with buttercream frosting. Stack the other on top. Freeze for 2 hours. Carve into a wedge shape and crumb-coat (see p.29). Allow to set for 1 hour.

2 On a surface dusted with cornstarch, roll out the lilac fondant to a ¼in (4mm) thick. Cover the cake, smoothing the fondant with the fondant smoother. Cut off the excess, and tuck the edges under the cake. Move the cake to the covered cake drum. Smooth with the fondant smoother before adding detail. Add shallow creases to the bag with the veining tool.

3 Cut a square with a rounded edge from more lilac fondant, to form the flap for the bag. To create the semicircle shape, cut around the edge of the round cake board,. For the quilting pattern, quilt with the stitching tool at 1in (2.5cm) intervals. Moisten the back of the flap with a little water and fix to the front of the cake.

4 To make the handles, roll out the black gum paste on a flat surface dusted with cornstarch and cut 2 strips measuring 8in (20cm) by 1⅓in (3.5cm). Stitch around the edges of each strip with the stitching tool.

BRING IT ALL TOGETHER

Carving and covering cakes *see p.65*

Modeling embellishments *see pp.96–97*

Quilting *see p.156*

Ingredients

* 9in (23cm) two-layer square vanilla sponge cake (see p.228), leveled and filled with vanilla buttercream (see p.28)
* ⅓ cup vanilla buttercream frosting (see p.24)
* cornstarch, for dusting
* 3lb 3oz (1.5kg) lilac fondant
* 2oz (50g) black gum paste
* 2oz (50g) black fondant, strengthened (see p.87)
* 2oz (50g) gray gum paste
* silver luster dust
* grain alcohol or vodka
* 1oz (25g) royal icing, for sticking
* edible glue

Tip

To make a charm, model a bow from black fondant. Make a thin rope with the gray fondant and join it around the handles. Make a single half-link and attach it to the top of the bow. Paint the chain with luster dust mixed with grain alcohol.

5 Turn the strips over and moisten the backs with water. Fold and then press together the strips, leaving 2in (5cm) flat at each end. Arrange in a semicircle and allow to dry overnight.

6 To make the black trim, roll a thin rope of black strengthened fondant with your hands, making it as long as you can. Run the fondant smoother over the rope to make it smooth and even. Work on one section at a time, making sure the rope is long enough to trim the section of the bag you are working on. Brush a little water around the edge of the bag and the flap, and fix the black rope to it.

7 Roll out another thin rope of gray gum paste, and cut it into about 15 pieces, each about 3in (7cm) in length. Wet one end and join together to form a link, smoothing the seam between your thumb and forefinger. Link with the next piece of fondant rope, repeating until you have a chain long enough to run down one side of the cake and spill out onto the board.

8 Attach the chain to one side of the handbag with a little water, starting from the top and carefully working downward. Repeat on the other side of the cake, making a chain of the same length and attaching it to the cake.

9 To join the lengths of chains on the board, roll out a black fondant shoulder strap (about 4 x 1½in/10cm x 3cm). Stitch each side with the stitching tool. Use a piping tip (PME no. 4) to cut out 2 circles for the chain to go through. Create another link for both of the chains, and thread them through the hole on each side of the strap. Mix the silver luster dust with grain alcohol and paint the chains. If you get paint on the cake, dip a cheesecloth in some grain alcohol and dab it off.

10 When the handles are dry, attach them onto the cake with a little royal icing. Put a support under the handles to keep them upright while the royal icing dries.

11 Use the end of the piping tip (PME no. 4) to cut 4 circles from the black fondant. Attach them to the handles with a little water. Paint with the silver luster dust mixed with some grain alcohol. Glue the ribbon around the covered drum, making sure to place the seam at the back of the drum. Dot the seam with royal icing.

Handbag cake pp.202–03

Blossom stencil cake pp.206–07

Blossom stencil cake

This delightful, two-tiered sponge cake is wrapped in white fondant and adorned with pretty fondant blossoms. A simple pattern of stripes is stenciled around the bottom tier in fuchsia royal icing.

⏰ **TIMING** allow 2 days, including drying time

 **SERVES** 20

Equipment

- 2 x round cake boards: 7in (17.5cm) and 5in (12.5cm) in diameter
- fondant roller
- striped stencil
- masking tape
- 4 dowels
- multi-ribbon cutter, straight edges
- small blossom plunger cutter
- flower mat or foam
- ball tool
- piping bag
- small piping tip (such as PME no. 0 or no. 1)

1 Two days before you want to serve, place each cake on its board and crumb-coat each one with a thin layer of buttercream frosting (see p.29). Let set overnight.

2 Roll out a sheet of white fondant on a surface dusted with confectioner's sugar and cover the largest cake and board. Smooth carefully and repeat with the smaller cake and board. Set aside. Let the cakes set for 1–2 days.

3 Scoop up any excess white fondant and strengthen with tylose powder (see p.87). Rest, covered in plastic wrap, for 24 hours until it is pliable.

4 When the fondant on the larger cake is dry, stencil the cake. Use a ruler to mark about ½in (1cm) down from the top of the cake, and prick the surface of the cake lightly at this point, all around, as a guide for the stencil.

5 Working around the cake, hold the stencil against the surface and apply masking tape to hold it in place. Smooth over the pink royal icing with a palette knife, working in one direction. Allow each section to dry a little before moving the

BRING IT ALL TOGETHER

Stenciling the sides of a cake see p.125

Building tiered cakes see p.68

Using multi-ribbon cutters see p.118

Using petal dusts see p.136

Ingredients

* 7in (17.5cm) round vanilla sponge cake (3 x 1in/2.5cm leveled layers, sandwiched with buttercream, see p.28)
* 5in (12.5cm) round vanilla sponge cake (2 x 1in/2.5cm leveled layers, sandwiched with buttercream, see p.28)
* ⅔ cup buttercream frosting (see p.24)
* 2lb 2oz (1kg) white fondant
* confectioner's sugar, for dusting
* tylose powder
* ½ cup pink royal icing (see p.34)
* cornstarch, for dusting
* 3½oz (100g) pink fondant, strengthened (see p.87)
* orange petal dust
* pink petal dust
* ¼ cup white royal icing, for piping (see pp.34–35)
* fresh flowers, preferably edible, to decorate

stencil and stenciling again. Continue until the whole circumference is stenciled. Touch up any uneven areas with a paintbrush dipped in a little water.

6 Insert the dowels, cut to size, into the larger cake (see p.68), and place the smaller cake and board on top, making sure to center it. Secure with royal icing or buttercream.

7 Dust a surface with a little cornstarch, and roll out the pink fondant to about ¼in (5mm) thick. Use the ribbon cutter to cut a ribbon the same length as the circumference of the cake, plus about ¹⁄₁₆in (a few millimeters) more. It should be about 20in (50cm) long and 1in (2.5cm) wide.

8 Dip a paintbrush in a little water and moisten a line around the base of the smaller cake, about 1in (2.5cm) up the cake. Carefully wrap the ribbon around the base of the cake, where it has been moistened, by rolling it up loosely and then unrolling it as you apply it to the cake.

9 Roll out the strengthened white fondant (from step 3) on a dusted surface to about ¹⁄₁₆in (2mm) thick. Lightly dust the surface of the fondant with cornstarch and use a small blossom plunger cutter to cut out about 25 blossoms.

10 Place the blossoms on the flower mat and use a ball tool to soften and thin the edges, curling the petals. Let them dry for about 10 minutes.

11 Brush half of the blossoms with orange petal dust and the other half with pink petal dust. Attach a small tip such as PME no. 0 or no. 1 to the piping bag and fill with white royal icing. Pipe little beads or dots into the center of each blossom (see p.80). Attach the tumbling blossoms to the cake with a little more royal icing.

12 For a final vibrant touch, decorate the top tier with bright fresh flowers that complement the colors of the blossoms.

Suitcase cake

Say "Bon voyage" or celebrate a special vacation with this suitcase, complete with hand-stitched trim, metallic painted fastenings, and, if desired, edible travel stickers printed with images of your favorite vacation destinations.

TIMING allow 1½ days, including drying time  **SERVES** 40

Equipment

* fondant roller
* cutting wheel
* 11in (28cm) rectangular fondant-covered drum
* multi-ribbon cutter
* stitching (quilting) tool
* small round piping tip
* circle cutters: ¾in (2cm) and ⅝in (1.5cm)

Ingredients

* cornstarch, for dusting
* 5lb 8oz (2.5kg) brown fondant
* 2 sponge cakes: 7in x 11in (18cm x 28cm) sandwiched and crumb-coated with buttercream (see p.29)
* 7oz (200g) lilac fondant, strengthened (see p.87)
* 2oz (50g) each of yellow and dark brown fondant, strengthened (see p.87)
* gold luster dust, mixed into paint (see p.136)

1 On a cornstarch-dusted surface, roll out the brown fondant to a large rectangle that is ⅛in (3mm) thick. Cover the cake with the fondant (see p.50). Mark a line halfway up the cake (about 2in/5cm) from the base, and use a cutting wheel to emboss a horizontal line. Transfer the cake to the covered cake board, so it sits toward the back. Let the cake set overnight.

2 Roll the lilac fondant to 1/16in (2mm) thick on a cornstarch-dusted surface. Use a ribbon cutter to cut two ½in (1cm) strips to run around the top and bottom edges of the cake. Fix to the cake around the base and on the top edge. Place the seam at the back. Use the stitching tool to detail both edges of the strips.

3 Roll out the strengthened yellow fondant and cut out 2 rectangles (1½in x 1in/4in x 2.5cm). Trim off the corners and use the piping tip to emboss 4 holes on each. Apply to the bottom half of the cake with water, 1in (2.5cm) in from each side. Cut 2 smaller yellow rectangles, 1in x ½in (2.5cm x 1cm) in size. Shape and emboss as above, and attach to the top half of the cake. Roll out 2 more rectangles, about ⅔in x ½in (1.5cm x 1cm) in size, and attach to the bottom half, 1½in (4cm) apart.

4 Cut out 2 circles using the large cutter, and 2 more using the small cutter. Moisten the backs with a little water and fix the large circles on the bottom plates and the small circles on top of these. Model 2 clasps and fix with water to the top and bottom plates. Paint the yellow fixings with the gold luster-dust paint.

5 Roll a sausage of strengthened dark brown fondant (⅔in x 6in/1.5cm x 15cm) to create a handle. Flatten and mark with the stitching tool. Attach to the suitcase, holding it in place for a few minutes so that it sticks. Attach images, if desired (see Tip).

Tip

Print edible images that are about 2¾in (7cm) in size (see pp.150–51). Peel off the backing paper and attach them to a sheet of white gum paste rolled to ⅛in (3mm) thick. Let dry. Cut out with a scalpel and attach to the suitcase with water.

BRING IT ALL TOGETHER

Using multi-ribbon cutters *see p.118*

Using petal dust *see p.136*

Using edible images *see pp.150–51*

Cigarillo wedding cake

This spectacular wedding cake is topped with modeled chocolate roses, wrapped in dark chocolate cigarillos, and embellished with chocolate ribbons. Styrofoam separates the layers to add height and allows you to tuck the roses neatly into the spaces below each tier.

CIGARILLO WEDDING CAKE **VARIATION:** WEDDING MINI CAKES *p.213*

 TIMING allow 1½ days, including drying time

SERVES 120 finger portions; 60 for dessert

Equipment

* fondant roller
* 13in (33cm) round cake drum
* 2 x Styrofoam separators: 5in x 1½in (12.5cm x 4cm) and 7in x 1½in (18cm x 4cm)
* rose petal cutters
* 9 dowels
* 2 x round cake boards: 6in (15cm) and 8in (20cm)
* multi-ribbon cutters, straight sides

1 A day before you want to serve the cake, on a flat surface dusted with confectioner's sugar, roll out a ball of dark chocolate fondant, strengthen with tylose powder (see p.87), and cover the cake drum (see p.51). Cover the 2 Styrofoam cake separators with the same fondant. Let dry overnight.

2 On the same day, model the roses using strengthened dark chocolate fondant. Make 55 medium chocolate roses, each about 2¼in (6cm) in diameter with about 12–15 petals (see p.88). Use the petal cutter to help. Allow to harden for at least 1 hour and up to 1 day. If you are making your own, prepare your cigarillos (see p.43), and allow to harden for at least 24 hours.

3 Place the largest frosted cake on the covered cake drum, fixing it with a little melted chocolate. Insert 5 dowels, cut to the height of the cake. Place the middle tier on its corresponding board, and insert 4 dowels, cut to the height of the cake. Place the top tier on its board and set aside.

METHOD CONTINUES · · · ·

BRING IT ALL TOGETHER

Modeling a fondant rose *see p.88*

Building tiered cakes *see p.68*

Using multi-ribbon cutters *see p.118*

Modeling embellishments *see p.96*

Tips

If desired, very gently steam the cake using an iron, about 4in (10cm) from the surface, or lightly spray with glaze (see p.159). Do not handle the cigarillos too much or they will become dull. A tip is to wear a pair of cotton gloves.

Ingredients

* confectioner's sugar, for dusting
* 6lb 8oz (3kg) dark chocolate fondant
* tylose powder
* 3lb (1.4kg) dark chocolate cigarillos (see p.43)
* 7oz (200g) dark chocolate, melted
* 3 x chocolate sponge cakes (see p.232): 4in (10cm), 6in (15cm), and 8in (20cm) in diameter, with three 1in (2.5cm) layers each; leveled, sandwiched, and frosted with chocolate buttercream frosting (see p.25, you'll need about 3 cups in total)
* 100g (3½oz) white chocolate clay (see pp.44–45)

4 Attach the chocolate cigarillos around the sides of each cake by gently pushing them into the buttercream frosting. Use more buttercream frosting, if required. Let dry for 30 minutes.

5 When the cigarillos are firmly attached to the cake, place the largest covered separator directly on top of the bottom tier, fixing it into place with melted chocolate. Place the middle tier on top of the separator, and fix it into place with melted chocolate.

6 Place the smaller separator on top of the middle tier of the cake, and attach with melted chocolate. This should be topped with the top tier of the cake, again fixed with chocolate.

7 Measure the circumference of the bottom tier (about 32in/81cm). On a surface dusted with confectioner's sugar, roll out the strengthened dark chocolate fondant to about ⅛in (3mm) thick. Prepare the ribbon cutter with straight sides and cut a ribbon with a width of 1¼in (3cm). It should be a little longer than the circumference of the cake. Set aside, keeping it flat.

8 Repeat for the middle and top tiers of the cakes, measuring each circumference and cutting a 1¼in- (3cm-) wide ribbon to the appropriate length. You should have 3 ribbons in all.

9 Roll out the white chocolate clay on a surface dusted with confectioner's sugar, to ⅛in (3mm) thick. Cut 3 ribbons the same length as the dark chocolate ones, but only ½in (1cm) wide. Lay the white chocolate ribbons on top of the dark chocolate ribbons of the same size, taking care to align them in the center of each. Gently rub to adhere.

10 Brush melted chocolate around the base of each cake tier and attach the ribbons in place over the chocolate.

11 On a surface dusted with confectioner's sugar, roll out another length of strengthened chocolate fondant to ⅛in (3mm). Use the ribbon cutter to create six 4in (10cm) lengths of ribbon, each 1¼in (3cm) wide. Form into bows, using extra fondant to create the center. Attach to the seam of the ribbon on each tier with chocolate. Decorate the top of the cake with the roses, using chocolate to adhere, and fill the spaces between the tiers with the chocolate roses.

CIGARILLO WEDDING CAKE **VARIATION**

Wedding mini cakes

Frosted with ganache, wrapped in chocolate fondant and finished with a pretty ribbon and chocolate roses, these gorgeous miniature wedding cakes make an ideal favor or sophisticated dessert. For completely edible cakes, cut your ribbons from white-chocolate clay instead (see opposite).

 **TIMING** allow 1½ days, including drying time

SERVES 12

Equipment

* fondant roller
* small rose leaf plunger cutter
* scraper, smooth-edged
* fondant smoother
* 8ft (2.5m) ivory grosgrain ribbon, ½in (12mm) wide

Ingredients

* 2lb 12oz (1.2kg) dark chocolate fondant
* tylose powder
* 12 x 3in (7cm) miniature round chocolate sponge cakes, halved and filled with chocolate buttercream frosting (see p.25)
* 3½ cups dark chocolate ganache (see p.38)
* confectioner's sugar, for dusting
* 2oz (50g) dark chocolate, melted
* edible glue

1 Strengthen 7oz (200g) of the dark chocolate fondant with tylose powder (see p.87) and allow to rest overnight. When the fondant is pliable, hand-model 12 small roses, 1in (2.5cm) wide. Set aside to dry for about 30 minutes. Roll out more strengthened fondant to ¹⁄₁₆in (2mm) thick and use the rose leaf plunger cutter to cut out 24 leaves. Curve the tips, and let dry for about 30 minutes. Use a palette knife to spread the sides and top of each cake with ganache. Run the scraper over the surface.

2 On a surface dusted with confectioner's sugar, roll out the remaining dark chocolate fondant to ⅛in (3mm) thick. Cut out 12 circles, large enough to cover the cakes, and smooth the fondant down over the cakes with a fondant smoother. Trim off any excess from the base. Rest for 30 minutes.

3 Use the melted chocolate to fix a rose and 2 leaves to the top of each cake. Cut the ribbon into 12 equal lengths, and wrap around the base of each cake, securing the seam with edible glue.

Filigree wedding cake

Beautifully piped with filigree lace and adorned with fondant roses, leaves, and appliqué blossoms, this exquisite, three-tiered cake is perfect for a wedding. Dress the cake with fresh edible flowers instead, if you like.

FILIGREE WEDDING CAKE **VARIATION:** BRIDAL LACE CUPCAKES *p.217*

TIMING allow 4 days, including drying time

SERVES 90–100 finger portions

Equipment

* 3 x cake boards: 4in (10cm), 8in (20cm), and 10in (25cm) in diameter
* fondant roller
* 18-gauge floral wire
* calyx cutter
* set of leaf plunger cutters
* ball tool
* rose leaf veiner
* template (see p.245)
* masking tape
* scribing tool
* turntable or lazy Susan
* small piping bags with tips (such as PME no. 1 and 3)

1 Four days before you want to serve the cake, place the fruitcakes on their boards and brush with apricot glaze. Dust a flat surface with confectioner's sugar, then roll out the marzipan. Cover the cakes (see p.37) and let dry overnight.

2 When the marzipan is dry, brush it with a little water. Roll out the white fondant to ⅛in (4mm) thick on a surface dusted with confectioner's sugar, and use to cover the cakes (see p.50). Trim off any excess and let the cakes rest for 2–3 days. Cover the remaining fondant with plastic wrap, and set aside.

3 Make sugar roses (see p.88) by forming 6–7 cones of fuchsia gum paste on 18-gauge floral wire. Place upright to dry for several days (see p.112). When the cones are dry, grease a surface with vegetable shortening and roll out the gum paste to 1/16in (1mm) thick. Model open roses over 5 of the dried cones. On the remaining cones, create rose buds with 5 petals. Roll a small ball of leaf-green gum paste and thread it onto the wire so that each cone has a base. Roll out more leaf-green fondant and then use the calyx cutter to cut calyxes. Slip them onto the base of the

METHOD CONTINUES • • • •

BRING IT ALL TOGETHER

Covering a cake with marzipan *see p.37*

Modeling a fondant rose *see p.88*

Piping filigree *see p.81*

Building tiered cakes *see p.68*

Tips

You could fix the roses onto a greased toothpick to dry, instead of wire. Lift off the dry roses and fix them onto the cake (step 10). Fix wired gum paste roses to the cake by pressing the wires into plastic flower picks (see p.18).

* small embossed blossom plunger cutter
* 13in (33cm) fondant-covered round cake drum (see p.51)
* 11 dowels
* 3ft (1m) white satin ribbon (½in/1cm wide)
* craft glue

Ingredients

* 3 x fruitcakes (p.233): 6in (15cm), 8in (20cm), and 10in (25cm) in diameter, each 3in (7.5cm) deep
* 10fl oz (300ml) apricot glaze (see p.37)
* confectioner's sugar, for dusting
* 4lb 8oz (2kg) marzipan
* 6lb 8oz (3kg) white fondant
* 7oz (200g) fuchsia gum paste
* vegetable shortening, for greasing
* 3½oz (100g) leaf-green gum paste
* edible petal dust in deep burgundy and pink
* 2 cups royal icing, for piping (see p.35)
* cornstarch, for dusting
* pearl luster dust
* grain alcohol or vodka

roses, pushing the wire through the center. Moisten and press onto the green ball at the base of the rose. Place on the stand to dry overnight. Once dry, dust the petal edges with a dark shade of petal dust and steam (see p.143). Allow to dry, and then carefully remove the wires, or insert into flower picks (see Tips, p.215).

4 Roll out the green gum paste to ¹⁄₁₆in (1mm) thick, cut the leaves using the rose-leaf veiner, and soften the edges with a ball tool. Dry overnight. Dust the edges with pink petal dust and steam. Allow to dry.

5 When the cakes are set, cut out scalloped-edge templates for all 3 tiers. Attach them around the tiers and hold in place with masking tape. Using a scribing tool, mark along the edge. Remove the templates and place the first cake on the turntable. Fill a piping bag with royal icing and attach a no. 1 tip. Outline the lace pattern by piping a scalloped line around the edge of the scribed template mark. Repeat for each cake.

6 On a cornstarch-dusted surface, roll out the remaining white fondant to ¹⁄₁₆in (1mm) thick, and cut out 18 blossoms using the plunger cutter. Fix to the scalloped sections with water.

7 When all the blossoms are applied, pipe the filigree infill in the remaining space. Repeat for each tier, and then pipe tiny, evenly spaced picot dots above the scallop outline on each cake.

8 Dowel the cakes, using 6 dowels for the bottom tier and 5 dowels for the top. Place the bottom tier, on its board, onto the covered cake drum, using royal icing to secure, and then stack the tiers on top (see p.68), securing each with royal icing.

9 Fill a piping bag with royal icing, and pipe a snail's trail (see p.80) around the base of each cake, using a no. 3 tip. Paint it with pearl luster dust mixed with grain alcohol.

10 Use royal icing to attach the roses to the cake, or, if still wired, press in the flower picks (see Tips, p.215). Cut a length of ribbon to fit around the base of the covered cake drum, and attach with double-sided tape or craft glue. Cover the seam with a series of piped picot dots.

FILIGREE WEDDING CAKE **VARIATION**

Bridal lace cupcakes

These cupcakes have royal icing filigree and a piped snail's trail painted with pearl luster dust. Ideal as wedding favors or a sweet treat to accompany a cake, they provide the perfect finishing touch for a special day. Measure the surface of the cupcakes first, to ensure that the fondant circles will cover the top exactly.

 TIMING 2 hrs   **MAKES** 12

Equipment

* fondant roller
* circle cutter, about 3in (7.5cm) in diameter
* small piping bag
* fine piping tips (such as PME no. 1 and 2)

Ingredients

* confectioner's sugar, for dusting
* 7oz (200g) white fondant
* 12 cupcakes (see p.240), lightly frosted with buttercream frosting (see pp.24–25)
* 2 cups royal icing, for piping (see p.35)
* edible pearl luster dust
* grain alcohol or vodka
* 12 edible diamonds

1 On a surface dusted with confectioner's sugar, roll out the white fondant to about ⅛in (3mm) thick and use the cutter to cut out 12 circles. Moisten the backs of the circles with water and place them on top of the cupcakes, smoothing them until flat.

2 Fit a no. 1 tip to a small piping bag and fill with royal icing. Pipe the surface of each cupcake with delicate filigree (see p.81). Leave a border of about 1⁄16in (2mm) around the outside of each fondant circle.

3 Fit a no. 2 tip to the piping bag and pipe delicate beading (see p.80) around the outside of the fondant circle. Allow to dry for 1 hour, or until hard.

4 Mix together some edible pearl luster dust with grain alcohol, and carefully paint the piped border. Place a dot of royal icing in the center of each cupcake and place an edible diamond on top.

Festive yule log

This rich, indulgent, and gloriously authentic Christmas yule log, complete with glistening snowflakes, is the perfect centerpiece for all winter celebrations. Rich chocolate buttercream frosting and marbled brown-and-white fondant create a feast for the eyes and the taste buds.

 TIMING allow 1½ days, including drying time    **SERVES** 10

Equipment

* snowflake plunger cutters
* 8in x 11in (20cm x 28cm) jelly roll pan, lined with parchment paper

Ingredients

* 2oz (50g) white fondant, strengthened (see p.87) and rolled out to ⅛in (3mm) thick
* 4 large eggs
* ½ cup granulated sugar
* 1 cup all-purpose flour
* 3 tbsp cocoa powder
* ½ tsp baking powder
* ¾ cup heavy cream
* 1 tsp pure vanilla extract
* 2 cups chocolate buttercream frosting
* 2oz (50g) each of 3 shades of brown fondant
* cornstarch, for dusting
* edible glitter
* confectioner's sugar, for dusting

1 Make the snowflakes a day before serving the log. Cut them out from the white fondant with the snowflake plunger cutters. Set aside on parchment paper to dry overnight.

2 Preheat the oven to 350°F (180°C). In a large bowl, beat together the eggs, sugar, and 1 tbsp of water. Beat for 5 minutes, until fluffy. Sift the flour, cocoa, and baking powder into the bowl, then fold into the egg mixture. Pour the mixture into the jelly roll pan and bake for 12 minutes, until springy to the touch. Meanwhile, using an electric mixer, beat the cream and vanilla extract on a high setting until you get soft peaks. Set aside.

3 Turn the cake onto a sheet of parchment paper, laid on a flat surface. Peel the paper from the back of the cake while still hot and then roll up the cake lengthwise into a tight roll, with the paper inside. Turn the log so that it sits on the seam. Cool.

4 Uncurl the log, remove the paper, and spread with the whipped cream. Reroll the cake and place on a plate with the seam-side down. Let set for 1 hour. Create a branch by cutting a quarter of the log off, at an angle, and placing it at the side. Gently warm the chocolate buttercream frosting to spreadable consistency and use a palette knife to cover the log. Use a fork to score patterns into the surface.

5 Form sausages with each shade of brown fondant and twist them together. Roll the twist out onto a surface dusted with cornstarch and fold and roll again until it is striped. Roll into a log and roll flat again, creating a spiral. Cut out 3 circles, then affix to the ends of the log and branch with buttercream. Dab the surface of the snowflakes with water and scatter with edible glitter. Use them to decorate the log, dusting it with confectioner's sugar.

Tip

Place the snowflakes on paper towels before sprinkling them with glitter. You can then collect any excess and pour it back into the container. Paint the surface of the snowflakes with edible pearl luster dust mixed with grain alcohol.

BRING IT ALL TOGETHER

Using plunger cutters
see pp.101–03

Working with edible glitter *see p.153*

Festive fruitcake

This simple yet elegant Christmas cake is covered in smooth royal icing and topped with a delicate robin run-out. Piped icicles decorate the top and a pretty fondant bow encircles the fruitcake, which can be made weeks in advance of your special celebration.

FESTIVE FRUITCAKE **VARIATION:** CHRISTMAS CAKE POPS p.223

TIMING allow 4 days, including drying time

SERVES 20

Equipment

* fondant roller
* robin templates (see p.244)
* masking tape
* food-grade acetate sheets
* piping bags with fine piping tips (such as PME no. 1 and 2)
* turntable or lazy Susan
* offset palette knife
* 12in (30cm) round cake drum, iced with royal icing
* multi-ribbon cutter, straight sides
* 3ft (1m) white satin ribbon (½in/1cm wide)
* craft glue

Ingredients

* confectioner's sugar, for dusting

1 Four days before you want to serve the cake, roll out the marzipan to ¼in (7.5mm) thick on an confectioner's-sugar dusted surface. Brush the surface of the cake with apricot glaze, and cover with marzipan (see p.37). Set aside to dry for 2–3 days. Trace the robin template on a sheet of paper. Use masking tape to secure it to a flat surface. Cover with acetate and secure with masking tape. Lightly grease the surface with shortening.

2 Place half of the piping-consistency royal icing in a bowl, double-wrap with plastic wrap, and set aside. Divide the remainder into four small pots. Use coloring paste to achieve the different colors for the robin.

3 Fit a small tip (no. 1) to each piping bag, and fill each with a different color. Using the right color for each part of the robin (e.g., yellow for the beak), pipe the outline of each part of the robin. Make sure that all the lines touch each other, as shown on p.140. Keep the piping bags upright with a wet sponge around the tip, to prevent them from drying out. Make a second outline for the robin's wing on a separate sheet of acetate. Let dry for a few hours. Decant each piping bag into its own bowl and cover tightly with plastic wrap. Set aside.

4 When the outlines are hard, thin the colored icings, one by one, with some water, adding a drop at a time until it reaches the right consistency. Transfer each icing batch to a piping bag fitted with a slightly bigger tip (no. 2), and begin your run-outs (see p.140). Allow each section to dry for about

METHOD CONTINUES • • • •

BRING IT ALL TOGETHER

Piping royal icing run-outs *see pp.140–41*

Piping dots, beads, and flowers *see p.80*

Using petal dusts *see p.136*

Modeling embellishments *see p.96*

* 1 batch marzipan
  (see p.36)
* 8in (20cm) fruitcake
  (see p.233)
* 3fl oz (90ml) apricot glaze
* vegetable shortening
* ¾ cup royal icing, for
  piping (see p.35)
* red, brown, yellow, and
  black coloring pastes
* 1 batch royal icing
  (see p.34)
* edible pearl luster dust
* cornstarch, for dusting
* 7oz (200g) red fondant,
  strengthened (see p.87)

10 minutes before moving on to another color. Fill in the second robin's wing in the same way. To achieve a good shine, allow to dry in a warm, dry place for several days.

5 While the robin run-out is drying, place the cake on a turntable. Apply a layer of royal icing (not piping consistency) to the marzipan with the palette knife, covering the sides first. Let dry, then apply another coat. Dry and add another layer of icing until the sides are lovely and smooth.

6 When the sides are dry, frost the top, following the same steps. Try to get a sharp edge where the sides meet the top. Let dry. Place the cake on the royal-iced cake drum, taking care to center it. Fill 2 piping bags and attach a no. 1 tip to one bag and a no. 2 tip to the other. Pipe a row of dots onto the surface of the cake, where the top meets the sides. Create icicles by piping dots that become a little smaller as you work down the cake in vertical lines. Make the lines uneven in length, to provide a more realistic effect. When dry, dust with pearl luster dust (see p.136).

7 Dust a flat surface with cornstarch, and roll out the red fondant to 1⁄16in (2mm) thick. Use the multi-ribbon cutter to cut a ribbon long enough to wrap around the base of the cake, ¾in (2cm) wide. Moisten the back and wrap around the cake with the seam at the front. Roll out another length of red fondant and create a bow (see p.96). Moisten the back and apply to the cake at the seam.

8 Very carefully lift the dry robin run-out from the acetate sheet, using a thin metal palette knife. You may have to move the knife gently from side to side to release it. Affix to the center of the cake with a small dot of royal icing. Dot a little royal icing onto the robin's wing portion of the run-out, and then carefully lift the second robin's wing on top, guiding it into place with your fingers. Allow to dry for about an hour.

9 Glue the satin ribbon around the base of the frosted cake drum, using craft glue. Pipe a few icicle dots over the seam at the back of the cake.

Tip

To create bauble mini cakes, form 2in (5cm) cake-pop balls (see p.242), and brush with jam. Wrap 4½oz (125g) of fondant around each ball, smoothing, cutting off excess, and then rolling in your hands. Cover with festive fondant decorations.

FESTIVE FRUITCAKE **VARIATION**

Christmas cake pops

Guaranteed to bring a smile, these delightful Christmas cake pops are a wonderful way to offer a sweet treat or party favor with a minimum of fuss. Use dabbed water to fix on your fondant decorations. To finish, you can wrap a length of ribbon around the stick of each cake pop.

 TIMING allow ½ day, including drying time

MAKES 16 (8 of each design)

Equipment

* 16 cake-pop sticks
* fondant roller
* small piping bag with fine tip (such as PME no. 1)

Ingredients

* 2oz (50g) brown gum paste
* 1oz (25g) each brown, black, orange, and white fondant, strengthened (see p.87)
* 16 un-dipped cake pops, stick inserted (see p.242)
* 14oz (400g) white chocolate melts
* 7oz (200g) milk chocolate melts
* 3½oz (100g) red fondant, strengthened (see p.87)
* ¼ cup royal icing, for piping (see p.35)
* edible white petal dust
* edible pink petal dust
* 2oz (50g) green fondant
* edible black pen

1 Make 16 antlers with pea-sized balls of brown gum paste. Roll into 1½in (4cm) sticks with pointed ends. Knead the orange fondant into 8 carrots, shaping peppercorn-size pieces into cones and scoring the surface. Allow the shapes to dry.

2 When dry, dip half the cake pops in melted white chocolate melts and press the carrot noses into the surface while soft. Dip the rest in the melted milk chocolate melts and press the antlers into the surface. Set the pops upright, to harden.

3 Use the brown and red fondant to decorate the reindeer. Score the smile with a piping tip, and use white and black fondant for the eyes, adding a piped royal icing gleam.

4 Dust the snowmen with edible white petal dust and a little edible pink petal dust for the cheeks. Use red and green fondant to model hats and the holly. Roll tiny balls of black fondant for the eyes. Create a smile with the edible black pen.

Ruffled cake

This elegant celebration cake is decorated with rows of fondant ruffles in ascending shades of blue, and topped with a wrapped fondant rose. Before you decorate the cake, cover the cake drum with fondant that has been strengthened with tylose powder (see p.51).

TIMING 1½ days, including drying time

SERVES 20 finger portions

Equipment

* 9in (23cm) fondant-covered cake drum (p.51)
* fondant roller
* multi-ribbon cutter, straight sides
* frilling tool
* 3 decorative stamens
* 3ft (1m) teal satin ribbon (½in/1cm wide)
* craft glue

Ingredients

* 2 x 6in (15cm) vanilla sponge cakes (see p.228), halved and layered with buttercream (see p.28)
* 1lb 2oz (500g) white fondant and 9oz (250g) white gum paste, kneaded together
* 1 tub blue coloring paste
* cornstarch, for dusting
* ⅔ cup buttercream frosting (see pp.24–25)
* edible glue

1 A day before serving, transfer the cake onto the covered cake drum. Divide the fondant–gum paste into 5 equal portions. Dip a toothpick into the coloring paste and add 1 dot to a portion. Knead it in. Add 2–3 dots of coloring paste to the second portion, and blend, ensuring the color is deeper than the previous portion. Continue with the final 3 portions, adding increasing amounts of coloring paste to create darker shades (i.e., 4–5 dots for the third portion, 7–8 dots for the fourth, and ½ tsp for the last). Wrap all of the fondant in plastic wrap.

2 On a cornstarch-dusted surface, roll out a small amount of the darkest blue fondant to ¹⁄₁₆in (2mm) thick and cut a strip about 1in (2.5cm) wide with a ribbon cutter. Use a frilling tool to frill one side of the strip. Moisten the unfrilled side and affix to the base of the cake with buttercream frosting. Repeat until a row of dark-blue ruffles surrounds the base of the cake.

3 Create a second layer of ruffles and work upward around the cake using the rest of the darkest fondant, finishing with a full row. Use the next shade of fondant and continue ruffling until the entire cake is covered. Use the lightest shade to create 2 layers around the top and a circle of ruffles on the cake's surface. Let the cake rest for a day, and start to model the flower.

4 Knead together the remaining fondant for an even color. Roll it out on a cornstarch-dusted surface to ¹⁄₁₆in (2mm) thick. Cut a 1½in x 12in (4cm x 30cm) strip, and gather it to model a flower shape, rolling until the flower is 4in (10cm) wide. Pinch together the fondant at the base and remove excess. Press the stamens into the center of the flower and let dry overnight. Attach to the top of the cake with a little edible glue. Use craft glue to secure the ribbon around the cake drum.

BRING IT ALL TOGETHER

Using multi-ribbon
cutters *see p.118*

Modeling
embellishments *see p.97*

CAKE BASICS

Anyone can bake truly delicious cakes. Here are all of the classic recipes—from light sponge cakes, lush pound cakes, rich fruitcakes, and moist gingerbread, to miniature cakes, cupcakes, and cake pops. Learn how to bake, test, cool, and level the perfect cake—a flawless canvas for decorating.

Classic vanilla sponge cake

This sponge cake makes a good base for many kinds of cake, and can be adapted to incorporate other flavors. Filled with jam and cream, for instance, it becomes a Victoria sponge cake. Use larger pans for thin layers and smaller pans for deeper ones.

PREP 20 mins　　**COOK** 25-30 mins　　**SERVES** 10

Equipment

* 2 x 8in (20cm) round cake pans, greased and lined (see p.236)

Ingredients

* scant 1 cup unsalted butter, softened
* ¾ cup granulated sugar
* 4 large eggs
* 1 tsp pure vanilla extract
* 1⅓ cups self-rising flour
* 1 tsp baking powder

Variations

A few extra ingredients can transform a basic sponge cake into something really special. Experiment with other flavors and textures. Add poppy seeds to a lemon sponge cake, or try flavored fruit and nut extracts like strawberry or almond.

1 Preheat the oven to 350°F (180°C). Beat the butter and sugar in a bowl for 2 minutes, or until pale and fluffy.

2 Add the eggs, 1 at a time, mixing well. Add the vanilla extract and beat for 2 minutes, until bubbles appear on the surface.

3 Sift in the flour and baking powder, and gently fold in with a metal spoon, keeping the mixture light and smooth.

To bake

Divide the mixture between the pans. Smooth the top. Bake in the lower third of the oven for 25–30 minutes, or until a skewer comes out clean (see p.238).

To finish

Cool the cakes in the pans for a few minutes, then turn onto a wire rack. When completely cool, fill as desired.

Coffee sponge cake

Coffee cake is a popular celebration cake and a traditional choice for brunch. The only additional ingredient you will need is some strong instant coffee, but you can add walnuts for even more flavor and texture.

Ingredients

* all ingredients for classic vanilla sponge cake plus:
* 1 tbsp strong instant coffee granules
* ½ cup chopped walnuts, optional
* coffee buttercream frosting (see p.25)

1 Mix together the strong instant coffee granules with 1 tablespoon of boiling water until dissolved. Allow to cool.

2 Follow steps 1–3 of the classic vanilla sponge cake recipe, opposite, then stir in the cooled coffee mixture. If desired, add the walnuts at the same time, and mix.

3 Continue to follow the recipe. When the cake has cooled, fill and frost with coffee buttercream frosting (see p.25).

Walnuts are flavorsome and can also be used for decorating.

Lemon sponge cake

A surprisingly light variation of the classic vanilla sponge cake, this is an ideal cake for the summer months. The lemon zest and juice add a tangy touch that cuts through the sweetness well.

Ingredients

* all ingredients for classic vanilla sponge cake, minus the vanilla extract, plus:
* finely grated zest and juice of 1 lemon
* lemon curd and lemon buttercream frosting (see p.25), optional

1 Follow steps 1–3 of the classic vanilla sponge cake recipe, but stir in the lemon zest and juice in place of the vanilla extract. If you like a particularly strong flavor, zest 2 lemons instead of 1, but use the same amount of lemon juice.

2 Continue to follow the recipe. When the cake has cooled, fill with lemon curd and frost with lemon buttercream frosting (see p.25).

Lemon provides a welcome tart contrast to sweet coverings.

Carrot cake

This rich, moist cake is not only easy to make, but also works well in stacked and layered projects because its density helps support additional weight. Cream cheese buttercream frosting (see p.25) is the perfect topping. Begin by toasting the walnuts and rubbing them to remove the skins.

 PREP 20 mins   **COOK** 45 mins   **SERVES** 10

Equipment

* 9in (23cm) round springform cake pan, greased and lined (see p.236)

Ingredients

* 1 cup walnuts
* 1 cup sunflower oil
* 3 large eggs
* 1 cup packed light brown sugar
* 1 tsp pure vanilla extract
* 1¼ cups grated carrots, about 7oz (200g)
* ¾ cup golden raisins
* 1⅓ cups self-rising flour, sifted
* ⅓ cup whole wheat flour, sifted
* pinch of salt
* 1 tsp ground cinnamon
* 1 tsp ground ginger
* ¼ tsp grated nutmeg
* grated zest of 1 orange

1 Preheat the oven to 350°F (180°C). Toast the walnuts for 5 minutes, rub with a dish towel, and chop roughly.

2 Pour the oil and eggs into a bowl and add the sugar and vanilla extract. Beat until smooth and thick.

3 Squeeze dry the carrots, and fold into the batter, followed by the walnuts and golden raisins. Stir in the remaining ingredients.

To bake

Spread in the pan, and smooth the top. Bake in the lower third of the oven for 50–60 minutes, or until a skewer comes out clean (see p.238).

To finish

Cool for 10 minutes in the pan. Transfer to a wire rack to cool completely. If desired, split and fill, or frost the top with cream cheese buttercream frosting (see p.25).

Pound cake

Just a few simple ingredients are needed to create this dense, buttery, lemon-flavored cake, which is ideal for carving and shaping. If you prefer, replace the lemon zest with 1½ teaspoons of pure vanilla extract or any other flavor of your choice.

 PREP 20 mins   **COOK** 50-60 mins   **SERVES** 10

Equipment

* 7in (18cm) round springform cake pan or 9in x 5in (23cm x 12cm) loaf pan, greased and lined (see p.236)

Ingredients

* ¾ cup unsalted butter, softened
* ¾ cup granulated sugar
* 3 large eggs
* 1½ cups self-rising flour
* grated zest of 1 lemon

Tip

Make sure you use the very best extracts you can find to flavor your cake. Pure extracts will always have a deeper, more natural taste than synthetic flavorings, and that can make all the difference to the finished cake.

1 Preheat the oven to 350°F (180°C). Beat the butter and sugar until fluffy. Mix in the eggs, one at a time.

2 Mix for 2 minutes more, until bubbles appear on the surface. Sift in the flour, add the zest, and fold in until just smooth.

3 Spoon into the pan and bake in the lower third of the oven for 50–60 minutes, or until a skewer comes out clean (see p.238). Let cool in the pan for 10 minutes and then turn onto a wire rack to cool completely.

Chocolate cake

Chocolate cake is an all-time favorite and the yogurt in this recipe makes it extra moist. If you like rich cakes, add another ¼ cup of cocoa powder and use crème fraîche in place of yogurt. This cake is delicious with a chocolate or vanilla buttercream frosting (see pp.24–25).

PREP 30 mins   **COOK** 20-25 mins   **SERVES** 10

Equipment

* 2 x 7in (18cm) round cake pans, greased and lined (see p.236)

Ingredients

* ¾ cup unsalted butter, softened
* ¾ cup packed light brown sugar
* 3 large eggs
* ¾ cup self-rising flour
* ½ cup cocoa powder
* 1 tsp baking powder
* 2 tbsp Greek yogurt
* chocolate buttercream frosting (see p.25)

1 Preheat the oven to 350°F (180°C). Beat the butter and sugar in a bowl until light and fluffy.

2 Add the eggs one at a time, beating after each addition. In a separate bowl, sift together the rest of the dry ingredients.

3 Fold the flour mixture into the batter, until well blended. When the batter is light and fluffy, gently fold through the yogurt.

To bake

Divide the mixture between the pans, smoothing the surface with a palette knife. Bake for 20–25 minutes, or until a skewer comes out clean (see p.238).

To finish

Cool the cakes in the pans for 5 minutes. Turn onto a wire rack. When cool, fill with chocolate buttercream frosting (see p.25).

Traditional fruitcake

This rich, dense cake is a popular choice for weddings and festivities. It also provides a strong base for stacked and layered cakes, and covers well with marzipan and royal icing, or fondant. Allow enough time to soak the fruit overnight at room temperature.

 PREP 25 mins   **COOK** 2½ hrs  **SERVES** 16

Equipment

* 10in (25cm) deep, round springform cake pan, greased and lined (see p.236)

Ingredients

* 1⅓ cups golden raisins
* 1⅓ cups raisins
* 2½ cups prunes, chopped
* 2¼ cups candied cherries
* 2 small apples, peeled, cored, and diced
* 2 cups sweet cider
* 4 tsp pumpkin pie spice
* scant 1 cup unsalted butter, softened
* ¾ cup packed dark brown sugar
* 3 large eggs, lightly beaten
* 1⅓ cups ground almonds
* 2 cups all-purpose flour
* 2 tsp baking powder

1 Simmer the first 7 ingredients in a large pot for 20 mins, until most liquid is absorbed. Remove from the heat. Let soak overnight.

3 Gently fold in the fruit mix and almonds. Sift over the rest of the dry ingredients and fold in, keeping the batter light and fluffy.

2 Preheat the oven to 325°F (160°C). Beat the butter and sugar until fluffy. Mix in the eggs, one at a time.

To bake

Spoon the mixture into the pan; cover with foil. Bake for 2 hours. Uncover; bake for ½ hour, or until a skewer comes out clean (see p.238).

To finish

Let cool in the pan for 10 minutes, then turn onto a wire rack to cool completely. If desired, pour a tablespoon of brandy or whiskey over the cake.

Red velvet cake

This vivid red cake is traditionally topped with cream cheese buttercream frosting. Boiled beets are used here in place of coloring paste to give the cake its signature color, but you can stir one teaspoon of red coloring paste in with the beets, if desired.

 PREP 30 mins   **COOK** 1½ hrs    **SERVES** 10

Equipment

* 2 x 8in (20cm) round cake pans, greased and lined (see p.236)

Ingredients

* 3–4 medium beets, 1lb 2oz (500g) in total
* 2¼ cups all-purpose flour
* ½ cup cocoa powder
* 2 tsp baking soda
* ½ tsp salt
* 12 tbsp unsalted butter, softened
* 1¼ cups packed brown sugar
* ¾ cup granulated sugar
* 3 large eggs, at room temperature
* 2 tsp pure vanilla extract
* 3½oz (100g) dark chocolate, broken into pieces and melted
* ⅔ cup buttermilk mixed with 2 tsp cider vinegar

1 Cook the beets in a pan covered with water for 30–40 minutes. Cool, then peel. Preheat the oven to 350°F (180°C).

2 Purée the beets in a food processor, adding a little water if necessary. Sift together the flour, cocoa, baking soda, and salt.

3 In a separate bowl, beat the butter, sugars, eggs, and vanilla, then add the cooled, melted chocolate.

To bake and finish

Slowly add the flour mixture and buttermilk–vinegar mix to the batter. Beat well between additions. Stir in 1 cup of the beet purée, and continue to mix. Divide the batter between the pans. Bake in the lower third of the oven for 35–45 minutes, or until a skewer comes out clean (see p.238). Let cool, slice each cake in half, and layer with cream cheese buttercream frosting (see p.25), if desired.

Gingerbread

Firm gingerbread is ideal for creating 3-D projects with a template. Before you begin building, allow at least a week for the gingerbread to harden. Gingerbread creations are traditionally "glued" together with royal icing (see pp.34–35) or melted, caramelized sugar (see Tip).

 PREP 30 mins    **COOK** 15 mins   **MAKES** 1¾lb (800g)

Ingredients

* ¾ cup corn syrup
* 8 tbsp butter, softened
* ½ cup brown sugar
* 4½ cups all-purpose flour, sifted, plus extra for dusting
* 1 tsp ground cinnamon
* 4 tsp ground ginger
* 4 tsp baking soda, dissolved in 4 tsp cold water
* 2 large egg yolks

Tip

To make sugar "glue," melt 1 cup white granulated sugar in a heavy-bottomed pan over medium heat, until the sugar melts and browns. Be careful, since it can burn. Spread onto the gingerbread edges to glue pieces together. Beware: it is very hot.

1 Melt the syrup, butter, and sugar in a pan. In a bowl, sift together the flour, cinnamon, and ginger. Make a well in the center.

2 Stir in the baking soda mix, yolks, and melted syrup, sugar, and butter. Knead into a pliable dough on a flour-dusted surface.

To shape

Place the template on top of the rolled-out dough, and cut around it using a sharp knife (see p.57).

3 While the dough is still warm, roll it out to about ¼in (5mm) thick. Preheat the oven to 350°F (180°C).

To bake

Carefully lift onto a lightly greased and lined baking sheet. Bake for 10–13 minutes, or until firm and just beginning to brown at the edges. Remove from the oven and cool on the sheet until required.

Preparing pans

Even the most perfectly baked cakes can be ruined if they stick to the cake pan, so it is essential that you prepare and line the pans properly. This will ensure that your cake can be removed in a smooth manner and cleaning-up time will be reduced considerably.

Greasing

Almost all cake pans, including nonstick pans, should be greased with butter, margarine, or oil. Use a pastry brush to ensure even coverage. Silicone pastry brushes are much more hygienic and easier to maintain than nylon or bristle brushes. Molded pans, especially novelty pans (see opposite), need to be greased very well in the corners and crevices.

Dusting

Pans without a nonstick coating must be dusted with flour after greasing. Sprinkle 1 tablespoon of all-purpose flour into the bottom of the pan. Hold the pan over the sink, tilt it to move the flour from side to side, and tap the bottom to ensure even coverage. Discard excess flour by inverting the pan and tapping the bottom.

Lining

Using parchment paper helps to prevent burning, particularly for cakes with longer cooking times.

1 Grease the pans to ensure that the parchment paper sticks to the pan and does not move when the batter is poured.

2 Cut a strip of parchment that is slightly longer than the circumference and slightly wider than the height of the pan.

3 Fold the strip about 1in (2.5cm) from the long edge and make some evenly spaced cuts to the fold line.

4 Press the parchment strip into the pan. Cut a circle, using the bottom of the pan as a template, and lay in the bottom of the pan.

Using a molded cake pan

Molded, novelty cake pans come in a variety of shapes, from simple 3-D balls to miniature wedding cakes, beehives, giant cupcakes, cars, and sand castles. If you are not confident enough to carve (see p.65), this is an ideal way to achieve the shape you want with minimum fuss.

Ball pans

For basic sponge cakes, grease and dust the pans. Lay them flat on a baking sheet and fill nearly to the top with batter. Make sure both halves are level, using scrunched-up foil to support. Bake according to instructions on the pan. Allow both halves to cool for 10 minutes in the pan, before trimming uneven edges and turning onto a wire rack. When cool, sandwich together with buttercream frosting (see p.28).

For denser batters, prepare the pans, as above, but fill only one pan half, creating a ball shape with your fingers that comes out over the top of the pan. Lock over the other half, and bake it on a baking sheet, as above. Cool in the pan, then turn the whole cake onto a wire rack to cool completely.

Novelty pans

1 After greasing and dusting, pour the batter into the pan so that it is just over three-quarters full. Tap it on a firm surface to release air bubbles and ensure a smooth finish.

2 Bake according to the instructions on the pan. It helps to place the novelty pan on a baking sheet for easy removal from the oven, and to catch any overspill while baking. Allow the cake to cool for at least 10 minutes in the pan before running a knife between the cake and the edge of the pan.

3 Gently turn the cake upside down on a wire rack, and lift the pan off the cake. If the cake has risen unevenly, or the surface of the cake domes in the center, level it (see p.239) before turning it out.

Baking and cooling

Make sure that cakes are cooked at the right temperature and for the correct length of time before you remove them from the oven. This ensures good consistency and optimum rising. It is also crucial to cool the cakes completely before frosting, filling, or decorating.

Baking

Preheat the oven for 20 minutes before baking. Fan or convection ovens require a lower temperature. If the recipe does not specify this, reduce the temperature by about 25°F (20°C). Knock the pan gently against a hard surface before it goes into the oven, to release air bubbles. Don't open the oven—changes in temperature cause cakes to sink. If your oven heats unevenly, turn the cake after three-quarters of the cooking time. Cook for the entire time suggested by the recipe.

Testing

There are two main ways to test a cake. The first is to press gently down in the center of the cake with your finger. If it springs back, chances are it is ready. To be certain, insert a metal or wooden skewer into the center of the cake (put it into a crack to keep from blemishing the surface). If it comes out clean, the cake is ready. Novelty cakes can take longer to bake, so be sure to check the recommended time on the recipe on the packaging.

Cooling

Cool a cake in its pan for about 10 minutes (a little longer if it is a deep, large cake), helping the cake to keep its shape and "set." Turn it onto one wire rack, and then invert it onto another rack to cool completely. The bottom of your cake should be on the rack, not the top, to prevent it from losing its height and texture. Always make sure the cake is cool before frosting and plating it, since this will prevent crumbling, breakage, and movement. If you are in a rush, you can chill your cake after it has been cooled in the pan.

Leveling

For a perfect finish, it is important to level the cake. If there are only a few uneven pieces, wait until the cake has cooled in the pan for 10 minutes, then gently trim them off with a knife. If the cake is lopsided or lumpy, let it cool completely on a wire rack before leveling it.

Turntable method

Place the cake on a cake board, and then on top of a turntable or lazy Susan. If it is not the board you will be using for the finished cake, dust it first with confectioner's sugar to ensure that the cake will not stick. Use a ruler and toothpicks pressed into the cake to mark your cutting line, to be sure it is even all the way around. Carefully turn the stand and gently move a serrated knife back and forth in a sawing motion to remove the dome. Some people find it easier to freeze the cakes partially before leveling, which prevents chunks of cake from being drawn up when you "saw" through it.

Cake leveler method

If you have a cake leveler, place the cake on a cake board, over a firm surface, and carefully position the blade at the appropriate height. Gently saw into the side using a back and forth motion. Once you have gotten past the crust, simply glide the blade through the cake to the other side. If you are finding it tricky to keep the cake still while you cut, you can place it on a board exactly the same size as the cake, and put the cake, on the board, back into the cake pan. Level across the cake using the top edge of the pan.

Making cupcakes

Be sure to fill the pans or paper liners properly and cook for the correct length of time. Always preheat the oven for at least 20 minutes. Prepare the pans before you begin to make the batter, so that it doesn't begin to rise before you put it into the paper liners.

Using paper liners

Cupcake paper liners add a decorative element, make the cupcakes look neater, and help them remain fresh and moist for longer. If you choose to use a cupcake pan on its own, grease and dust it, brush with cake release products, or spray with a nonstick baking spray. Silicone cases do not require a cupcake pan. Fill and set them upright on a baking sheet. Grease and dust them with all-purpose flour to ensure that the cupcakes do not stick.

Filling

Fill the cupcake paper liners or pans about two-thirds full. Do not overfill or they can spill over the sides or develop a "nose." Standard-sized cupcakes require about ¼ cup batter. For mini cupcakes, a heaping tablespoon of batter is enough. For special effects, layer different colors of batter into the paper liners with a piping bag. Create a surprise center by placing candies or even a cookie or miniature brownie into the center before baking.

Baking

A standard-sized cupcake will take 18–20 minutes to bake, while mini cupcakes will take 8–10 minutes. They are ready if a skewer inserted in the middle of the cupcake comes out clean. When baking several pans at the same time, increase the baking time by a few minutes, and rotate the sheets halfway through. Let cool in the pan for at least 10 minutes and then cool on a wire rack. If you do not use paper liners, turn the cupcakes onto your hand before placing them on the rack.

Baking miniature cakes

Make miniature ("mini") cakes in the same way as cupcakes, but bake them in specially designed round or square cake pans. Grease and dust the pans carefully. You could use deep cutters or a knife to cut mini cakes from a large cake, but this is not as accurate and you may waste cake.

 PREP 20 mins   **COOK** 15 mins   **MAKES** 16

Equipment

* 16 x 2in (5cm) mini round cake pans

Ingredients

* 1 batch pound cake batter (see p.231)

1 Preheat the oven to 375°F (190°C). Fill all of the pans with the same amount of batter—roughly half to two-thirds full.

2 Mini cakes take 15–25 minutes to bake, depending on their size, so check the instructions on the cake pan.

3 When they look like they may be done, test every two minutes until a skewer comes out clean (see p.238). Let cakes to cool in the pans and then turn onto a wire rack.

Tips
Bake cupcakes as soon as the batter is ready. This will ensure that the air in the mixture does not escape, resulting in flatter cupcakes. Cupcakes and mini cakes can be decorated, once cool, with a variety of toppings (see pp.32–33).

Divide the mix *equally among the pans. Trim the cakes when they have cooled, if necessary.*

Making cake pops

Cake pops are relative newcomers to the baking arena and offer a perfect opportunity to accessorize cakes, create a decorative theme (see p.223). There are two ways to make cake pops. This method uses of leftover cake that you can form into balls, hearts, or other shapes.

 PREP 4 hrs   **MAKES** 20-25

Equipment

* 25 cake-pop sticks
* floral foam or Styrofoam

Ingredients

* 4 cups chocolate cake crumbs (½ batch chocolate cake batter p.232)
* ½ cup chocolate buttercream frosting (see p.25)
* 9oz (250g) dark chocolate almond bark
* 2oz (50g) white chocolate
* 10oz (300g) candy melts (optional, to replace dark and white chocolate)
* sprinkles, nuts, or ground wafers, to decorate, optional

1 Place the cake crumbs in a large bowl, and stir in the buttercream frosting, mixing until you have a smooth dough.

2 Using your hands, gently mold the mixture into uniform balls, each the approximate size of a walnut.

3 Place on a plate, with space between each, and refrigerate for 3 hours; alternatively, you can freeze for 30 minutes.

To cover

Line two baking sheets with parchment paper and melt some chocolate almond bark. Dip one end of a cake-pop stick into the chocolate and insert into the center of each pop. Cool for 30 minutes, standing upright in the floral foam. Melt the remaining almond bark and white chocolate, or candy melts. Dip the balls in and swirl to cover. Let the excess drip off then dip in sprinkles, nuts, or ground wafers, if desired.

Using a cake-pop pan

Cake-pop pans look like miniature "ball pans" (see p.237). Use them to create uniform balls that are ready to dip and decorate. Light sponge cakes are not dense enough to support the weight of the pop on a stick, or the decorations. Pound cake is a better option. Most cake-pop pans come with recipes.

 PREP 20 mins   **COOK** 15–18 mins   **MAKES** 12

Equipment

* 12-hole cake-pop pan

Ingredients

* all-purpose flour, to dust
* ½ batch pound cake batter (see p.231)
* melted chocolate

1 Preheat the oven to 350°F (180°C). Grease and dust the pans. Spoon the batter into the bottom half of the pan (without holes) so that it mounds over the top of the pan. Every cake-pop pan is different, so follow the specific instructions to ensure you use the correct amount of batter.

2 Place the top half of the pan on top and secure with keys. Bake for 15–18 minutes. After baking time, test every two minutes until a skewer comes out clean. Allow the cakes to cool in the pan for 10 minutes and then turn onto a wire rack to cool completely.

3 Chill the cake pops before decorating, so that they to keep their shape. First, dip one end of a cake-pop stick into a little melted chocolate and insert into the center of each pop. Chill for 20–30 minutes, with the sticks upright. Cover, as described opposite.

Cool cake pops in the pan before inserting the cake-pop sticks.

Tip

To keep the chocolate or candy melts warm and in a liquid state while dipping, use a fondue pot or place the pan on a tea-light burner. Using a taller, narrow pan makes dipping easier and much less messy.

Templates

Templates ensure that you have an accurate pattern for 3-D constructions and decorations. You can enlarge or reduce the scale of them to suit the size of any cake. Each of the templates here has an enlargement percentage that will help you to scale them to individual projects.

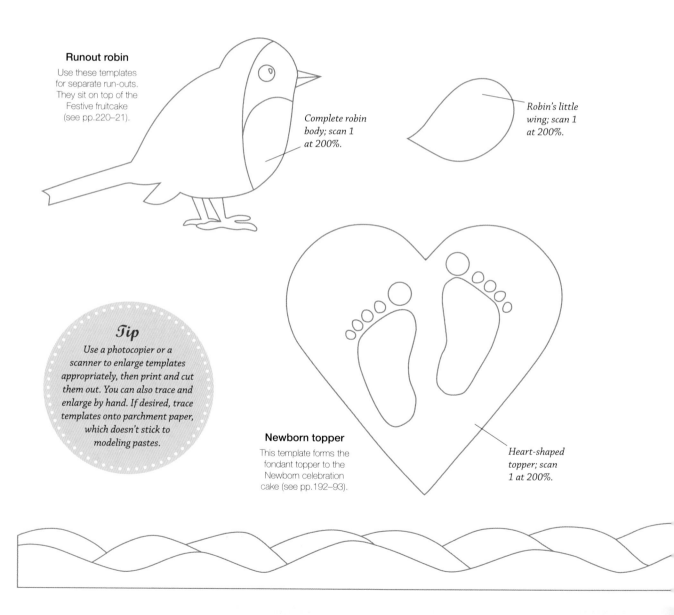

Runout robin

Use these templates for separate run-outs. They sit on top of the Festive fruitcake (see pp.220–21).

Complete robin body; scan 1 at 200%.

Robin's little wing; scan 1 at 200%.

Tip

Use a photocopier or a scanner to enlarge templates appropriately, then print and cut them out. You can also trace and enlarge by hand. If desired, trace templates onto parchment paper, which doesn't stick to modeling pastes.

Newborn topper

This template forms the fondant topper to the Newborn celebration cake (see pp.192–93).

Heart-shaped topper; scan 1 at 200%.

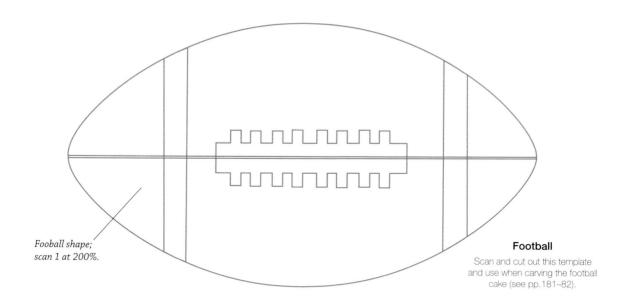

Fooball shape; scan 1 at 200%.

Football

Scan and cut out this template and use when carving the football cake (see pp.181–82).

Scalloped-edge marker

Scan, cut out, and tape together multiples of this template so that every tier on the Filigree wedding cake (see pp.214–16) has a template to mark the top of the filigree piping.

Scalloped-edge marker; scan multiples at 200%.

Princess garden template; scan 1 at 400%.

Princess garden marker

Scan, cut out, and use to measure out the rolling fields around the Princess castle cake (see pp.170–75).

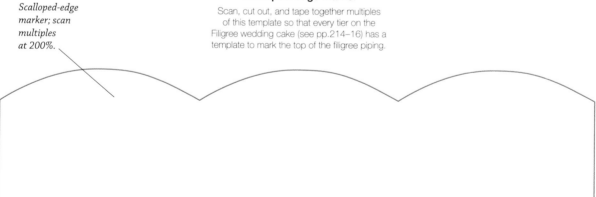

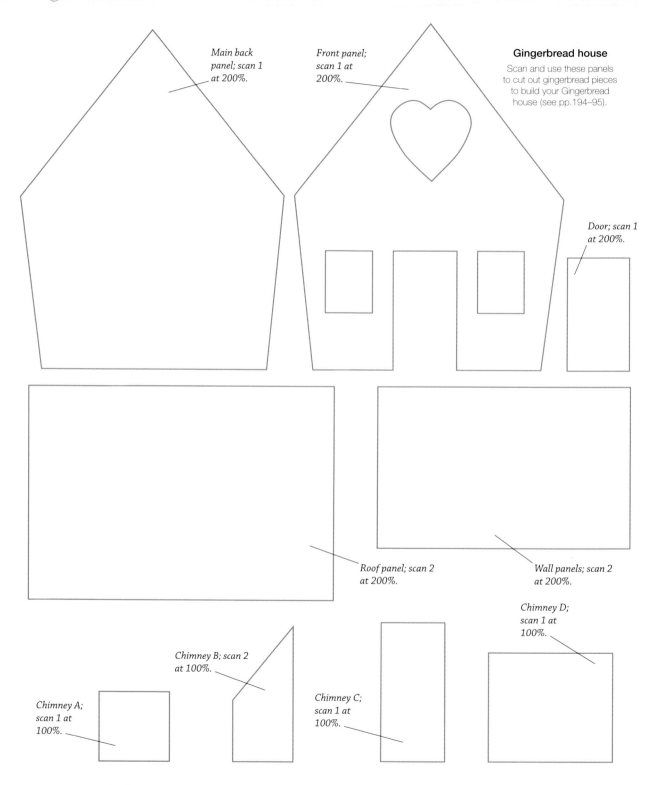

Main back panel; scan 1 at 200%.

Front panel; scan 1 at 200%.

Gingerbread house

Scan and use these panels to cut out gingerbread pieces to build your Gingerbread house (see pp.194–95).

Door; scan 1 at 200%.

Roof panel; scan 2 at 200%.

Wall panels; scan 2 at 200%.

Chimney D; scan 1 at 100%.

Chimney B; scan 2 at 100%.

Chimney A; scan 1 at 100%.

Chimney C; scan 1 at 100%.

About the contributors

Karen Sullivan is a writer, editor, and custom cake-maker with a successful celebration cake business in London, UK. She learned to bake as a toddler, in her grandmother's kitchen in Canada, and has honed her decorating skills over the years. She creates unique and highly sought-after cakes for a range of occasions.

Asma Hassan is the owner of The Sugared Saffron Cake Company, specializing in modern wedding cakes and dessert tables. She is a self-taught cake decorator whose work features in bridal and sugarcraft publications.
Her work features on p.1; pp.4–5; p6; p.7 (Teddy bear mini cakes); p.23 (Butterfly cupcakes); p.45; p.54; p.72; pp.76–77; p.100; p.124; p.163; pp.184–85 (Butterfly cupcakes); pp.190–91; pp.196–97; pp.198–201; pp.205–07; pp.210–13; and pp.224–25.

www.sugaredsaffron.co.uk

Sandra Monger is an award-winning cake designer based in Bath, UK, who specializes in custom wedding and celebration cakes. Professionally trained in advanced pâtisserie and sugarcraft, she also teaches cake-decorating courses. Her work features on p.2; p.7 (Princess cake pops); p.23 (Blossom cupcakes); pp.26–27; p.32; pp.38–39; p.43; p.55; p.56; p.85; p.86; pp.92–93; p.97 (ruffles); p.141; p.147; p.148; p.152; p.156; p.162; pp.170–75; pp.180–83; pp.184–85 (Blossom cupcakes); pp.192–93; pp.194–95; pp.208–09; pp.214–17; pp.220–23; p.226; p.227; and p.247.

www.sandramongercakes.co.uk

Amelia Nutting is an award-winning cake decorator and owner of Shuga Budz, a family-run cake decorating company based in Wolverhampton, UK. For the last six years she has been entering national decorating competitions and teaching courses to decorating enthusiasts of all ages.
Her work features on p.3; p.22; pp.82–83; pp.90–91; pp.94–95; pp.104–05; p.109; pp.132–33; p.134; p.143; pp.164–66; pp.167–69; pp.176–79; pp.202–04; and pp.218–19.

www.facebook.com/shuga.budz

Adapting cake quantities

To adapt recipes for cakes of any size and shape, multiply the batches of batter you make. Test cakes regularly to make sure they are perfectly baked—large cakes require the most time.

Cake pan	Multiple of basic fruitcake recipe	Cooking time for fruitcake recipe at 325°F (160°C)	Marzipan to cover	Multiple of basic sponge cake recipe	Cooking time for sponge cake recipe at 350°F (180°C)
ROUND CAKE PANS					
5 x 2½in (13 x 6cm)	1	2¼–2¾ hrs	12oz/340g	1	15–20 mins
6 x 2½in (15 x 6cm)	1	2¾–3¼ hrs	1lb/450g	1	20–35 mins
7 x 2¾in (18 x 7cm)	1½	3½–4 hrs	1¼lb/570g	1½	30–35 mins
8 x 3in (20 x 7.5cm)	2	4–4½ hrs	1½lb/680g	2	35–40 mins
9 x 3¼in (23 x 8cm)	2½	4¼–4¾ hrs	2lb/900g	2½	40–45 mins
10 x 3½in (25.5 x 9cm)	3	5–5½ hrs	2½lb/1.1kg	3½	50–55 mins
11 x 3¾in (28 x 9.5cm)	4	5½–6 hrs	3lb/1.3kg	–	–
12 x 4in (30 x 10cm)	5	6–6½ hrs	3lb 3oz/1.5kg	–	–
14 x 4½in (35.5 x 11.5cm)	6	6¾–7¼ hrs	4lb/1.8kg	–	–
SQUARE CAKE PANS					
6 x 2½in (15 x 6cm)	1½	3½–4 hrs	1½lb/680g	1½	30–35 mins
7 x 2¾in (18 x 7cm)	2	4–4½ hrs	1¾lb/800g	2	35–40 mins
8 x 3in (20 x 7.5cm)	2½	4¼–4¾ hrs	2lb/900g	2½	40–45 mins
9 x 3¼in (23 x 8cm)	3	5–5½ hrs	2½lb/1.1kg	3½	50–55 mins
10 x 3½in (25.5 x 9cm)	4	5½–6 hrs	2¾lb/1.25kg	5	60–65 mins
11 x 3¾in (28 x 9.5cm)	5	6¼–6¾ hrs	3lb 3oz/1.5kg	–	–
12 x 4in (30 x 10cm)	6	6¾–7¼ hrs	4lb/1.8kg	–	–
14 x 4½in (35.5 x 11.5cm)	7	7½–8 hrs	4½lb/2kg	–	–
HEART CAKE PANS					
6 x 3in (15 x 7.5cm)	1½	3–3½ hrs	1¼lb/570g	1½	30–35 mins
12 x 4½in (30 x 11.5cm)	6	6–6½ hrs	3¾lb/1.7kg	–	–
HEXAGON CAKE PANS					
6 x 2½in (15 x 6cm)	1	2¾–3¼ hrs	1lb/450g	1	25–30 mins
8 x 3¼in (20 x 8cm)	2	4–4½ hrs	1½lb/680g	2	35–40 mins
10 x 3½in (25.5 x 9cm)	3	5–5½ hrs	2½lb/1.1kg	3½	50–55 mins
12 x 4in (30 x 10cm)	5	6–6½ hrs	3lb 3oz/1.5kg	–	–
OVAL CAKE PAN					
8 x 6¼in (20 x 16cm)	1½	3–3½ hrs	1lb/450g	1½	30–35 mins
10 x 8in (25.5 x 20cm)	2½	4¼–4¾ hrs	1½lb/680g	3	40–45 mins
12 x 10in (30 x 25.5cm)	4	5¼–5¾ hrs	2¼lb/1kg	–	–

Resources

US RESOURCES

Bake It Pretty
A great stop for beginning bakers. Specializing in cake decorating kits to get you started, with piping bags, tips, food coloring, and more.
196 Sugar Street, #4
Layton, Utah 84041
www.bakeitpretty.com

Baking Addict Supplies
A one-stop online shop for all things cake pop.
www.bakingaddict.com

Cake Arts
Offering a full selection of decorating supplies, from chocolate to sprinkles, and even how-to videos.
2853 E. Indian School Road
Phoenix, Arizona 85016
www.cakearts.com

Cake Central
A fantastic cake forum where members share ideas, advice, and reviews. A good resource for tips on where to find the best, often most elusive, products. The site includes a blog, tutorials, and online shop.
www.cakecentral.com

Confectionary House
An online store with a wealth of cake decorating ideas and the supplies to create them.
975 Hoosick Road
Troy, New York 12180
www.confectioneryhouse.com

Fancy Flours
A dazzling array of themed caked decorations and novelty pans.
705 Osterman Drive, Suite E
Bozeman, Montana 59715
www.fancyflours.com

Global Sugar Art
An expansive array of fondant, pastes, and molds.
1509 Military Turnpike
Plattsburgh, New York 12901
www.globalsugarart.com

Kitchen Krafts
Cake decorating supplies for the hobbyist and professional. Online store features cake pans, pastry bags, coloring pastes, decorating tubes, fondant molds, recipes, and decorating advice.
www.kitchenkrafts.com

Jo-Ann
A nationwide chain with a wide selection of bakeware, decorating tools, and ingredients. Shop online or check the store locator. Classes available.
www.joann.com

Michael's
North America's largest specialty retailer of arts and crafts supplies, with a full line of bakeware products and tools, and decorating supplies. In-store events and classes, how-to videos, online bookstore, and a vibrant online community. Shop online or visit the website's store locator to find a store nearby.
www.michaels.com

Shop Bakers Nook
A huge selection of cake decorating supplies and a great blog offering the latest ideas in cake decorating from leading bakers and cake decorators.
901 West Michigan Avenue
Saline, Michigan 48176
www.shopbakersnook.com

Sugarcraft
Offering over 30,000 baking and decorating products, Sugarcraft also makes edible prints from personal photos.
3665 Dixie Highway
Hamilton, Ohio 45015
www.sugarcraft.com

Sweet Estelle's Baking Supply
An online-only store with colorful, vintage-inspired baking supplies, from pastry bags to sprinkles to fun cupcake liners. A free newsletter features the latest products, recipes, and discounts available.
www.sweetestelle.com

The Baker's Kitchen
Specializing in edible decorations like gem stones, diamonds, pearl dragées, and glitters, The Baker's Kitchen stocks everything for baking and candy-making.
6433 Monclova Road
Maumee, Ohio 43537
www.thebakerskitchen.net

US Cake Supply
An online company stocking virtually every cake-decorating product available, from airbrushing systems to bakeware to petal dusts, fondants, and pastes. The site also features a learning section with recipes, patterns, and resources.
www.uscakesupply.com

Wilton
A comprehensive one-stop shop offering everything from supplies to cake-decorating classes, recipes, a blog, and online demos. Wilton products are also available from other retailers and online suppliers.
Wilton Homewares
7511 Lemont Road
Darien, Illinois 60561
www.wilton.com

CANADIAN RESOURCES

Cake Mischief
A comprehensive selection of cake decorating supplies like crimpers, cutters, and impression mats.
5540 163rd Ave
Edmonton, Alberta T5Y 3L3
www.cakemischief.com

Canadian Cake Decorators Guild
Membership is open to both hobbyists and professionals. It offers discounts, group meetings, and access to an online community.
www.canadiancakedecorators.com

Design and Realisation
Offering one of the largest selections of pastry rings, chocolate molds, chocolate transfer sheets, and tempering machines.
2620 Lapierre
Montreal, Quebec H8N 2W9
www.dr.ca

Flour Confections
Lots of airbrush accessories, dowels, pillars, and supports for all types of cake.
1084 Brock (Salk) Road, Unit 5
401 Brock Court
Pickering, Ontario L1W 4B6
www.flourconfections.com

Golda's Kitchen
The leading Canadian online shopping site for specialty cake decorating supplies.
2885 Argentia Road, Unit 6
Mississauga, Ontario L5N 8G6
www.goldaskitchen.com

J. Wilton
A source for cake decorating and candy-making supplies, including tools, accessories, recipe idea books, and online video classes.
4746 76 Avenue NW
Edmonton, Alberta T6B 0A5
www.j-wilton.com

Phat Cat Cake Craft
A store offering supplies for cake decorating, plus a range of classes from decorating basics to more advanced techniques.
374 Main Street
Penticton, British Columbia V2A 5C3
www.phatcatcakes.com

Qzina
Offering baking supplies and decorating courses in Toronto, Edmonton, and Vancouver.
11851 Hammersmith Way,
Richmond, British Columbia V7A 5E5
www.qzina.com

Index

Page numbers in **bold** indicate step-by-step techniques and those in *italic* indicate complete cake projects.

Acknowledgments

The author would like to thank three of the most inspiring, delightful, and imaginative cake decorators around: Asma Hassan, Sandra Monger, and Amelia Nutting. Their help in producing gorgeous projects and advising on the techniques has been invaluable. I've learned more from them in four months than I have in five years of cake decorating. Thank you to the DK team, which has worked wonders to produce a lovely, dynamic, and truly helpful book; in particular, Martha Burley is probably the most organized, efficient, and accommodating editor on the face of the Earth; Kathryn Wilding has created a superb design and was forever willing to tinker in order to get in all the things we needed. Peggy Vance saw promise in the idea; Charis Bhagianathan, Janashree Singha, Dawn Henderson, and Christine Keilty helped it to come to fruition. Thank you all. Special thanks must go to Rosa Viacava, whose "RVO" lace molds were shipped from Peru to feature in this book.

DK Publishing would like to thank Karen Sullivan, Asma Hassan, Sandra Monger, and Amelia Nutting for their creative cake decorating and inspiration. Thanks also go to the following:

Photography Clive Bozzard-Hill
Additional photography William Reavell
Art direction Penny Stock
Home economist Paul Jackman
Prop styling Liz Hippisley
Proofreading Corinne Masciocchi and Sue Morony
Indexing Vanessa Bird
Design assistance Tessa Bindloss, Kate Fenton, Lucy Parissi, and Harriet Yeomans
Editorial assistance Elizabeth Clinton